The Pursuit of God

A 31-Day Experience

A 31-Day

EXPERIENCE

THE

PURSUIT

of

GOD

A.W. TOZER

Compiled by

EDYTHE DRAPER

Christian Publications
3825 Hartzdale Drive
Camp Hill, PA 17011

Faithful, biblical publishing since 1883
LOC Catalog Card Number: 95-71543
ISBN: 0-87509-615-8

95   96   97   98   99   5   4   3   2   1

Cover by Larry Smith and Associates, Inc.

Unless otherwise indicated, Scripture taken from the
HOLY BIBLE, AUTHORIZED
KING JAMES VERSION

Contents

Day 1

God Is Never Found Accidentally

Then shall we know, if we follow on to know the LORD: his going forth is prepared as the morning; and he shall come unto us as the rain, as the latter and former rain unto the earth.

Hosea 6:3

*C*hristian theology teaches the doctrine of prevenient grace, which, briefly stated, means that before a man can seek God, God must first have sought the man.

Before a sinful man can think a right thought of God, there must have been a work of enlightenment done within him. Imperfect it may be, but a true work nonetheless, and the secret cause of all desiring and seeking and praying which may follow.

We pursue God because, and only because, He has first put an urge within us that spurs us to the pursuit. "No man can

1

come to me," said our Lord, "except the Father which hath sent me draw him," and it is by this prevenient *drawing* that God takes from us every vestige of credit for the act of coming. The impulse to pursue God originates with God, but the outworking of that impulse is our following hard after Him. All the time we are pursuing Him we are already in His hand: "Thy right hand upholdeth me."

In this divine "upholding" and human "following" there is no contradiction. All is of God, for as von Hügel teaches, *God is always previous.* In practice, however (that is, where God's previous working meets man's present response), man must pursue God. On our part there must be positive reciprocation if this secret drawing of God is to eventuate in identifiable experience of the Divine. In the warm language of personal feeling, this is stated in Psalm 42:1-2:

The greatest need of the human personality is to experience God Himself. This is because of who God is and who and what man is.

—AWT in That Incredible Christian

> As the hart panteth after the water brooks, so panteth my soul after thee, O God. My soul thirsteth for God, for the living God: when shall I come and appear before God?

This is deep calling unto deep, and the longing heart will understand it.

The doctrine of justification by faith—a biblical truth, and a blessed relief from sterile legalism and unavailing self-effort—has in our time fallen into evil company and been interpreted by many in such a manner as actually to bar men from the knowledge of God. The whole transaction of religious conversion has been made mechanical and spiritless. Faith may now be exercised without a jar to the moral life and without embarrassment to the Adamic ego. Christ may be "received" without creating any special love for Him in the soul of the receiver. The man is "saved," but he is not hungry nor thirsty after God. In fact, he is specifically taught to be satisfied and is encouraged to be content with little.

There are two reasons for loving God:
no one is more worthy of our love,
and no one can return more
in response to our love.
—Bernard of Clairvaux

The modern scientist has lost God amid the wonders of His world; we Christians are in real danger of losing God amid the wonders of His Word. We have almost forgotten that God is a person and, as such, can be cultivated as any person can. It is inherent in personality to be able to know other personalities, but full knowledge of one personality by another cannot be achieved in one encounter. It is only after long and loving mental intercourse that the full possibilities of both can be explored.

All social intercourse between human beings is a response of personality to personality, grading upward from the most casual brush between man and man to the fullest, most intimate communion of which the human soul is capable. Religion, so far as it is genuine, is in essence the response of created personalities to the creating personality, God. "This is life eternal, that they might know thee the only true God, and Jesus Christ, whom thou hast sent" (John 17:3).

Tis not enough to save our souls,
To shun the eternal fires;
The thought of God will rouse the heart
To more sublime desires.

How little of that road, my soul!
How little hast thou gone!
Take heart, and let the thought of God
Allure thee further on.
—Frederick W. Faber

◊   ◊   ◊

Day 2

The Glorious Pursuit

God and man exist for each other and neither is satisfied without the other.
—*AWT in* That Incredible Christian

My soul followeth hard after thee: thy right hand upholdeth me.

Psalm 63:8

God is a person, and in the deep of His mighty nature He thinks, wills, enjoys, feels, loves, desires and suffers as any other person may. In making Himself known to us He stays by the familiar pattern of personality. He communicates with us through the avenues of our minds, our wills and our emotions. The continuous and unembarrassed interchange of love and thought between God and the soul of the redeemed man is the throbbing heart of New Testament religion.

This intercourse between God and the soul is known to us in conscious personal awareness. It is personal: It does not stay below the threshold of consciousness and

7

work there unknown to the soul (as, for instance, infant baptism is thought by some to do), but comes within the field of awareness where the man can know it as he knows any other fact of experience.

*We are called to an everlasting
preoccupation with God.*
—AWT *in* That Incredible Christian

You and I are in little (our sins excepted) what God is in large. Being made in His image we have within us the capacity to know Him. In our sins we lack only the power. The moment the Spirit has quickened us to life in regeneration our whole being senses its kinship to God and leaps up in joyous recognition. That is the heavenly birth without which we cannot see the kingdom of God. It is, however, not an end but an inception, for now begins the glorious pursuit, the heart's happy exploration of the infinite riches of the Godhead. That is where we begin, I say, but where we stop no man has yet discovered, for there is in the awful and mysterious depths of the Triune God neither limit nor end.

Shoreless Ocean, who can sound Thee?
Thine own eternity is round Thee,
  Majesty divine!

To have found God and still to pursue Him is the soul's paradox of love, scorned indeed by the too-easily-satisfied religionist, but justified in happy experience by the children of the burning heart. St. Bernard stated this holy paradox in a musical quatrain that will be instantly understood by every worshiping soul:

> We taste Thee, O Thou Living Bread,
>   And long to feast upon Thee still:
> We drink of Thee, the Fountainhead
>   And thirst our souls from Thee to fill.

Come near to the holy men and women of the past and you will soon feel the heat of their desire after God. They mourned for Him; they prayed and wrestled and sought for Him day and night, in season and out, and when they had found Him the finding was all the sweeter for the long seeking. Moses used the fact that he knew God as an argument for knowing Him better. "Now therefore, I pray thee, if I have found grace in thy sight, show me now thy way, that I may know thee, that I may find grace in thy sight" (Exodus 33:13); and from there he rose to make the daring request, "I beseech thee, show me thy glory" (33:18). God was frankly pleased by this display of ardor, and the next day called Moses into the mount, and there in solemn procession made all His glory pass before him.

David's life was a torrent of spiritual desire, and his psalms ring with the cry of the seeker and the glad shout of the finder. Paul confessed the mainspring of his life to be his burning desire after Christ. "That I may know him" (Philippians 3:10) was the goal of his heart, and to this he sacrificed everything. "Yea doubtless, and I count all things but loss for the excellency of the knowledge of Christ Jesus my Lord: for whom I have suffered the loss of all things, and do count them but dung, that I may win Christ" (3:8).

Hymnody is sweet with the longing after God, the God whom, while the singer seeks, he knows he has already found. "His track I see and I'll pursue," sang our fathers only a short generation ago, but that song is heard no more in the great congregation. How tragic that we in this dark day have had our seeking done for us by our teachers. Everything is made to center upon the initial act of "accepting" Christ (a term, incidentally, which is not found in the Bible) and we are not expected thereafter to crave any further revelation of God to our souls. We have been snared in the coils of a spurious logic which insists that if we have found Him, we need no more seek Him. This is set before us as the last word in orthodoxy, and it is taken for granted that no Bible-taught Christian ever believed otherwise. Thus the whole testimony of the worshiping, seeking, singing church on that subject is crisply set aside. The experiential heart-theology of a grand army of fragrant saints is rejected in favor of a smug interpretation of Scripture which would certainly have sounded strange to an Augustine, a Rutherford or a Brainerd.

I came to love You late, O Beauty so ancient and new; I came to love You late. You were within me and I was outside, where I rushed about wildly searching for You like some monster loose in Your beautiful world. You were with me, but I was not with You. You called me, You shouted to me, You wrapped me in Your splendor, You sent my blindness reeling. You gave out such a delightful fragrance, and I drew it in and came breathing hard after You. I tasted and it made me hunger and thirst; You touched me, and I burned to know Your peace.

—St. Augustine of Hippo

In the midst of this great chill there are some, I rejoice to acknowledge, who will not be content with shallow logic. They will admit the force of the argument, and then turn away with tears to hunt some lonely place and pray, "O God, show me Thy glory." They want to taste, to touch with their hearts, to see with their inner eyes the wonder that is God.

Make your heart a vacuum and the Spirit will rush in to fill it.
—AWT in Man: The Dwelling Place of God

I want deliberately to encourage this mighty longing after God. The lack of it has brought us to our present low estate. The stiff and wooden quality about our religious lives is a result of our lack of holy desire. Complacency is a deadly foe of all spiritual growth. Acute desire must be present or there will be no manifestation of Christ to His people. He waits to be wanted. Too bad that with many of us He waits so long, so very long, in vain.

> *O God, show me Thy glory, I pray Thee, that so I may know Thee indeed. Begin in mercy a new work of love within me. Say to my soul, "Rise up, my love, my fair one, and come away." Then give me grace to rise and follow Thee up from this misty lowland where I have wandered so long. In Jesus' name. Amen.*

Day 3

Discovering the Simplicity in Seeking God

And ye shall seek me, and find me, when ye shall search for me with all your heart.
                                    Jeremiah 29:13

For every one that asketh receiveth; and he that seeketh findeth; and to him that knock-eth it shall be opened.
                                    Luke 11:10

Sow to yourselves in righteousness, reap in mercy; break up your fallow ground: for it is time to seek the LORD, till he come and rain righteousness upon you.
                                    Hosea 10:12

*E*very age has its own characteristics. Right now we are in an age of religious complexity. The simplicity which is in Christ is rarely found among us. In its stead are pro-grams, methods, organizations and a world of nervous activities

13

which occupy time and attention but can never satisfy the longing of the heart. The shallowness of our inner experience, the hollowness of our worship and that servile imitation of the world which marks our promotional methods all testify that we, in this day, know God only imperfectly, and the peace of God scarcely at all.

> Let Him lead thee blindfold onwards,
>   Love needs not to know;
> Children whom the Father leadeth
>   Ask not where they go.
> Though the path be all unknown,
> Over moors and mountains lone.
>
> Give no ear to reason's questions;
>   Let the blind man hold
> That the sun is but a fable
>   Men believed of old.
> At the breast the babe will grow;
> Whence the milk he need not know.
>   —Gerhard Tersteegen

If we would find God amid all the religious externals, we must first determine to find Him and then proceed in the way of simplicity. Now, as always, God discovers Himself to "babes" and hides Himself in thick darkness from the wise and the prudent. We must simplify our approach to Him. We must strip down to essentials (and they will be found to be blessedly few). We must put away all effort to impress and come with the guileless candor of childhood. If we do this, without doubt God will quickly respond.

When religion has said its last word, there is little that we need other than God Himself. The evil habit of seeking *God-and* effectively prevents us from finding God in full revelation. In the *and* lies our great woe. If we omit the *and* we shall soon find God, and in Him we shall find that for which we have all our lives been secretly longing.

We need not fear that in seeking God only we may narrow our lives or restrict the motions of our expanding hearts. The opposite is true. We can well afford to make God our All, to concentrate, to sacrifice the many for the One.

The author of the quaint old English classic, *The Cloud of Unknowing*, teaches us how to do this.

> Lift up thine heart unto God with a meek stirring of love; and mean Himself, and none of His goods. And thereto, look thee loath to think on aught but God Himself. So that nought work in thy wit, nor in thy will, but only God Himself. This is the work of the soul that most pleaseth God.

Again, he recommends that in prayer we practice a further stripping down of everything, even of our theology. "For it sufficeth enough, a naked intent direct unto God without any other cause than Himself." Yet underneath all his thinking lay the broad foundation of New Testament truth, for he explains that by "Himself" he means "God that made thee, and bought thee, and that graciously called thee, to thy degree." And he is all for simplicity: If we would have religion

> God impoverishes only to make rich, becoming in secret Himself the substitute for all that He takes away from the soul.
> —Jeanne Guyon

lapped and folden in one word, for that thou shouldest have better hold thereupon, take thee but a little word of one syllable: for so it is better than of two, for even the shorter it is the better it accordeth with the work of the Spirit. And such a word is this word GOD or this word LOVE.

When the Lord divided Canaan among the tribes of Israel, Levi received no share of the land. God said to him simply, "I am thy part and thine inheritance," and by those words made him richer than all his brethren, richer than all the kings and rajas who have ever lived in the world. And there is a spiritual principle here, a principle still valid for every priest of the Most High God.

The man who has God for his treasure has all things in One. Many ordinary treasures may be denied him, or if he is allowed to have them, the enjoyment of them will be so tempered that they will never be necessary to his happiness. Or if he must see them go, one after one, he will scarcely feel a sense of loss, for having the Source of all things he has in One all satisfaction, all pleasure, all delight. Whatever he may lose he has actually lost nothing, for he now has it all in One, and he has it purely, legitimately and forever.

O God, I have tasted Thy goodness, and it has both satisfied me and made me thirsty for more. I am painfully conscious of my need of further grace. I am ashamed of my lack of desire. O God, the Triune God, I want to want Thee; I long to be filled with longing; I thirst to be made more thirsty still. In Jesus' name. Amen.

~Show Me Thy Face~

Show me Thy face—one transient gleam
　　Of loveliness divine,
And I shall never think or dream
　　Of other love save Thine:
All lesser light will darken quite,
　　All lower glories wane,
The beautiful of earth will scarce
　　Seem beautiful again.

Show me Thy face—my faith and love
　　Shall henceforth fixed be,
And nothing here have power to move
　　My soul's serenity.
My life shall seem a trance, a dream,
　　And all I feel and see
Illusive, visionary—Thou
　　The one reality!

Show me Thy face—I shall forget
　　The weary days of yore,
The fretting ghosts of vain regret
　　Shall haunt my soul no more.
All doubts and fears for future years
　　In quiet trust subside,
And naught but blest content and calm
　　Within my breast abide.

Show me Thy face—the heaviest cross
　　Will then seem light to bear;
There will be gain in every loss,
　　And peace with every care.
With such light feet the years will fleet,
　　Life seem as brief as blest,
Till I have laid my burden down,
　　And entered into rest.

　　　　　　　　　— Author Unknown

Day 4

The Tyranny of Things

A man's life consisteth not in the abundance of the things which he possesseth.

Luke 12:15

*B*efore the Lord God made man upon the earth He first prepared for him a world of useful and pleasant things for his sustenance and delight. In the Genesis account of the creation these are simply "things." They were made for man's use, but they were meant always to be external to the man and subservient to him. In the deep heart of the man was a shrine where none but God was worthy to come. Within him was God; without, a thousand gifts which God had showered upon him.

But sin has introduced complications and has made those very gifts of God a potential source of ruin to the soul.

Our woes began when God was forced out of His central shrine and things were allowed to enter. Within the human heart things have taken over. Men have now by nature no peace within their hearts, for God is crowned there no longer, but there in the moral dusk, stubborn and aggressive usurpers fight among themselves for first place on the throne.

This is not a mere metaphor, but an accurate analysis of our real spiritual trouble. There is within the human heart a tough, fibrous root of fallen life whose nature is to possess, always to possess. It covets *things* with a deep and fierce passion. The pronouns *my* and *mine* look innocent enough in print, but their constant and universal use is significant. They express the real nature of the old Adamic man better than a thousand volumes of theology could do. They are verbal symptoms of our deep disease. The roots of our hearts have grown down into *things,* and we dare not pull up one rootlet lest we die. Things have become necessary to us, a development never originally intended. God's gifts now take the place of God, and the whole course of nature is upset by the monstrous substitution.

> *Idolatry is not only the adoration of images . . . but also trust in one's own righteousness, works and merits, and putting confidence in riches and power.*
>
> —Martin Luther

Our Lord referred to this tyranny of things when He said to His disciples, "If any man will come after me, let him deny himself, and take up his cross, and follow me. For whosoever will save his life shall lose it: and whosoever will lose his life for my sake shall find it" (Matthew 16:24–25).

Breaking this truth into fragments for our better understanding, it would seem that there is within each of us an enemy which we tolerate at our peril. Jesus called it "life" and "self," or as we would say, the *self-life*. Its chief characteristic is its possessiveness; the words *gain* and *profit* suggest this. To allow this enemy to live is, in the end, to lose everything. To repudiate it and give up all for Christ's sake is to lose nothing at last, but to preserve everything unto life eternal. And possibly also a hint is given here as to the only effective way to destroy this foe: It is by the cross. "Let him take up his cross, and follow me."

Hold loosely all that is not eternal.
—Agnes Maude Royden

~Tozer—Thoughts on the Cross~

It is easy to learn the doctrine of personal revival and victorious living; it is quite another thing to take our cross and plod on to the dark and bitter hill of self-renunciation.
—Born After Midnight

The cross would not be a cross to us if it destroyed in us only the unreal and the artificial. It is when it goes on to slay the best in us that its cruel sharpness is felt.
—Born After Midnight

To try to find a common ground between the message of the cross and man's fallen reason is to try the impossible, and if persisted in must result in an impaired reason, a meaningless cross and a powerless Christianity.
—That Incredible Christian

We must do something about the cross, and one of two things only we can do—flee it or die upon it.
—The Root of the Righteous

Our cross will be determined by whatever pain and suffering and trouble which will yet come to us because of our obedience to the will of God.
—I Talk Back to the Devil

Every advance that we make for God and for His cause must be made at our inconvenience. If it does not inconvenience us at all, there is no cross in it! If we have been able to reduce spirituality to a smooth pattern and it costs us nothing—no disturbance, no bother and no element of sacrifice in it—we are not getting anywhere with God.
—I Talk Back to the Devil

No one wants to die on a cross—until he comes to the place where he is desperate for the highest will of God in serving Jesus Christ.
—I Talk Back to the Devil

One of the reasons we exhibit very little spiritual power is because we are unwilling to accept and experience the fellowship of the Savior's sufferings, which means acceptance of His cross.
—I Talk Back to the Devil

In coming to Christ we do not bring our old life up onto a higher plane; we leave it at the cross. The corn of wheat must fall into the ground and die.
—Man: The Dwelling Place of God

The pain of the cross means that we are in the way.
—That Incredible Christian

Day 5

The Joy of Possessing Nothing

Blessed are the poor in spirit: for theirs is the kingdom of heaven.

Matthew 5:3

For thus saith the high and lofty One that inhabiteth eternity, whose name is Holy; I dwell in the high and holy place, with him also that is of a contrite and humble spirit.

Isaiah 57:15

Hath not God chosen the poor of this world rich in faith, and heirs of the kingdom which he hath promised to them that love him?

James 2:5

The way to deeper knowledge of God is through the lonely valleys of soul poverty and abnegation of all things. The blessed ones who possess the kingdom are they who have repudiated every external thing and have rooted from their hearts all sense of possessing. These are the "poor in spirit." They have reached an inward state paralleling the outward circumstances of the common beggar in the streets of Jerusalem. That is what the word *poor* as Christ used it actually means. These blessed poor are no longer slaves to the tyranny of things. They have broken the yoke of the oppressor; and this they have done not by fighting but by surrendering. Though free from all sense of possessing, they yet possess all things. "Theirs is the kingdom of heaven."

Let me exhort you to take this seriously. It is not to be understood as mere Bible teaching to be stored away in the mind along with an inert mass of other doctrines. It is a marker on the road to greener pastures, a path chiseled against the steep sides of the mount of God. We dare not try to by-pass it if we would follow on in this holy pursuit. We must ascend a step at a time. If we refuse one step, we bring our progress to an end.

As is frequently true, this New Testament principle of spiritual life finds its best illustration in the Old Testament. In the story of Abraham and Isaac we have a dramatic picture of the surrendered life as well as an excellent commentary on the first Beatitude.

Abraham was old when Isaac was born, old enough to have been his grandfather, and the child became at once the delight and idol of his heart. From the moment he first stooped to take the tiny form awkwardly in his arms, he was an eager love slave of his son. God went out of His way to comment on the strength of this affection. And it is not hard to understand. The baby represented everything sacred to his father's heart: the promises of God, the covenants, the hopes of the years and the long messianic dream. As he watched him grow from babyhood to young manhood, the heart of the old man was knit closer and closer with the life of his son, till at last the relationship bordered upon the perilous. It was then that God stepped in to save both father and son from the consequences of an uncleansed love.

"Take now thy son," said God to Abraham, "thine only son Isaac, whom thou lovest, and get thee into the land of Moriah; and offer him there for a burnt offering upon one of the mountains which I will tell thee of " (Genesis 22:2). The sacred writer spares us a close-up of the agony that night on the slopes near Beersheba when the aged man had it out with his God, but respectful imagination may view in awe the bent form wrestling convulsively alone under the stars. Possibly not again until One greater than Abraham

Better in bitterest agony to lie Before Thy throne, Than through much increase to be lifted up on high, And stand alone. Yet best—the need that broke me at thy feet, In voiceless prayer, And cast my chastened heart, a sacrifice complete, Upon Thy care.

—John Oxenham

27

wrestled in the Garden of Gethsemane did such mortal pain visit a human soul. If only the man himself might have been allowed to die. That would have been a thousand times easier, for he was old now, and to die would have been no great ordeal for one who had walked so long with God. Besides, it would have been a last, sweet pleasure to let his dimming vision rest upon the figure of his stalwart son who would live to carry on the Abrahamic line and fulfill in himself the promises of God made long before in Ur of the Chaldees.

How should he slay the lad! Even if he could get the consent of his wounded and protesting heart, how could he reconcile the act with the promise, "In Isaac shall thy seed be called"? This was Abraham's trial by fire, and he did not fail in the crucible. While the stars still shone like sharp white points above the tent where the sleeping Isaac lay, and long before the gray dawn had begun to lighten the east, the old saint had made up his mind. He would offer his son as God had directed him to do, and *then trust God to raise him from the dead*. This, says the writer to the Hebrews, was the solution his aching heart found sometime in the dark night, and he rose "early in the morning" to carry out the plan. It is beautiful to see that, while he erred as to God's method, he had correctly sensed the secret of His great heart. And the solution accords well with the New Testament Scripture, "Whosoever will lose . . . for my sake shall find" (Matthew 16:25).

God let the suffering old man go through with it up to the point where He knew there would be no retreat, and then forbade him to lay a hand upon the boy. To the wondering patriarch He now says in effect, "It's all right, Abraham. I never intended that you should actually slay the lad. I only wanted to remove him from the temple of your heart that I might reign unchallenged there. I wanted to correct the perversion that existed in your love. Now you may have the boy, sound and well. Take him and go back to your tent. Now I know that thou fearest God, seeing that thou hast not withheld thy son, thine only son, from Me."

If the cross suited us, it would no longer be a cross, and if we refuse those that hurt us, we will refuse all crosses. The cross which God sends us must of necessity always be humiliating, painful, paralyzing, difficult.

—Louis Evely

Then heaven opened and a voice was heard saying to him:

> By myself have I sworn, saith the LORD, for because thou hast done this thing, and hast not withheld thy son, thine only son: That

in blessing I will bless thee, and in multiply-
ing I will multiply thy seed as the stars of
the heaven, and as the sand which is upon
the sea shore; and thy seed shall possess the
gate of his enemies; And in thy seed shall all
the nations of the earth be blessed; because
thou hast obeyed my voice. (Genesis 22:16–
18)

The old man of God lifted his head to respond
to the Voice, and stood there on the mount strong
and pure and grand, a man marked out by the
Lord for special treatment, a friend and favorite of
the Most High. Now he was a man wholly surrendered, a man utterly obedient, a man who possessed nothing. He had concentrated his all in the
person of his dear son, and God had taken it from
him. God could have begun out on the margin of
Abraham's life and worked inward to the center.
He chose rather to cut quickly to the heart and
have it over in one sharp act of separation. In dealing thus, He practiced an economy of means and
time. It hurt cruelly, but it was effective.

I have said that Abraham possessed nothing.
Yet was not this poor man rich? Everything he
had owned before was his still to enjoy: sheep,
camels, herds and goods of every sort. He had also
his wife and his friends, and best of all he had his
son Isaac safe by his side. He had everything, *but*

he possessed nothing. There is the spiritual secret. There is the sweet theology of the heart which can be learned only in the school of renunciation. The books on systematic theology overlook this, but the wise will understand.

After that bitter and blessed experience I think the words *my* and *mine* never again had the same meaning for Abraham. The sense of possession which they connote was gone from his heart. Things had been cast out forever. They had now become external to the man. His inner heart was free from them. The world said, "Abraham is rich," but the aged patriarch only smiled. He could not explain it, but he knew that he owned nothing, that his real treasures were inward and eternal.

Fully surrendered, Lord, I would be,
Fully surrendered, dear Lord, to Thee.
All on the altar laid,
Surrender fully made,
Thou hast my ransom paid;
I yield to Thee.

Fully surrendered—life, time, and all,
All Thou hast given me held at Thy call.
Speak but the word to me,
Gladly I'll follow Thee,
Now and eternally
Obey my Lord.

Fully surrendered—silver and gold,
His, who hath given me riches untold.
All, all belong to Thee,
For Thou didst purchase me,
Thine evermore to be,
Jesus, my Lord.

       —A.C. Snead

Day 6

The Way of Renunciation

The dearest idol I have known,
Whate'er that idol be,
Help me to tear it from Thy throne,
And worship only Thee.

—*William Cowper*

There can be no doubt that this possessive clinging to things is one of the most harmful habits in the life. Because it is natural, it is rarely recognized for the evil that it is. But its outworkings are tragic.

We are often hindered from giving up our treasures to the Lord out of fear for their safety. This is especially true when those treasures are loved relatives and friends. But we need have no such fears. Our Lord came not to destroy but to save. Everything is safe which we commit to Him, and nothing is really safe which is not so committed.

Our gifts and talents should also be turned over to Him. They should be recognized for what they are, God's loan to us, and should never be considered in any sense our own. We have no more right to claim credit for special abilities than for blue eyes or strong muscles. "For who maketh thee to differ from another? and what hast thou that thou didst not receive?" (1 Corinthians 4:7).

The Christian who is alive enough to know himself even slightly will recognize the symptoms of this possession malady and will grieve to find them in his own heart. If the longing after God is strong enough within him, he will want to do something about the matter. Now, what should he do?

First of all, he should put away all defense and make no attempt to excuse himself either in his own eyes or before the Lord. Whoever defends himself will have himself for his defense, and he will have no other. But let him come defenseless before the Lord and he will have for his defender no less than God Himself. Let the inquiring Christian trample under foot every slippery trick of his deceitful heart and insist upon frank and open relations with the Lord.

> Who can understand his errors? cleanse thou me from secret faults. Keep back thy servant also from presumptuous sins; let them not have dominion over me.
>
> Psalm 19:12-13

Then he should remember that this is holy business. No careless or casual dealings will suffice. Let him come to God fully determined to be heard. Let him insist that God accept his all, that He take

34

things out of his heart and Himself reign there in power. It may be he will need to become specific, to name things and people by their names one by one. If he will become drastic enough, he can shorten the time of his travail from years to minutes and enter the good land long before his slower brethren who coddle their feelings and insist upon caution in their dealing with God.

Let us never forget that a truth such as this cannot be learned by rote as one would learn the facts of physical science. They must be *experienced* before we can really know them. We must, in our hearts, live through Abraham's harsh and bitter experiences if we would know the blessedness which follows them. The ancient curse will not go out painlessly; the tough old miser within us will not lie down and die in obedience to our command. He must be torn out of our heart like a plant from the soil; he must be extracted in agony and blood like a tooth from the jaw. He must be expelled from our soul by violence, as Christ expelled the money-changers from the temple. And we shall need to steel ourselves against his piteous begging and to recognize it as springing out of self-pity, one of the most reprehensible sins of the human heart.

If we would indeed know God in growing intimacy, we must go this way of renunciation. And if we are set upon the pursuit of God, He will sooner or later bring us to this test. Abraham's testing was, at the time, not known to him as such, yet if he had taken some course other than the one he did, the whole history of the Old Testament would have been different. God would have found His man, no doubt, but the loss to Abraham would have been tragic beyond the telling. So we will be brought one by one to the testing place, and we may never know when we are there. At that testing place there will be no dozen possible choices for us—just one and an alternative—but our whole future will be conditioned by the choice we make.

Father, I want to know Thee, but my cowardly heart fears to give up its toys. I cannot part with them without inward bleeding, and I do not try to hide from Thee the terror of the parting. I come trembling, but I do come. Please root from my heart all those things which I have cherished so long and which have become a very part of my living self, so that Thou mayest enter and dwell there without a rival. Then shalt Thou make the place of Thy feet glorious. Then shall my heart have no need of the sun to shine in it, for Thyself wilt be the light of it, and there shall be no night there. In Jesus' name. Amen.

~Rules for Self-Discovery~

1. What we want most
2. What we think about most
3. How we use our money
4. What we do with our leisure time
5. The company we enjoy
6. Who and what we admire
7. What we laugh at
   —*AWT in* That Incredible Christian

Self-knowledge is so critically important to us in our pursuit of God and His righteousness that we lie under heavy obligation to do immediately whatever is necessary to remove the disguise and permit our real selves to be known.
   —*AWT in* That Incredible Christian

[The Lord] will bring to light the hidden things of darkness, and will make manifest the counsels of the hearts.
                    1 Corinthians 4:5

He revealeth the deep and secret things: he knoweth what is in the darkness, and the light dwelleth with him.
                    Daniel 2:22

Day 7

Now the Journey Can Begin

*Whom have I in heaven but thee? and there
is none upon earth that I desire beside thee.*

Psalm 73:25

*With my soul have I desired thee in the
night; yea, with my spirit within me will I
seek thee early.*

Isaiah 26:9

Among the famous sayings of the church fathers, none is better known than Augustine's: "Thou hast formed us for Thyself, and our hearts are restless till they find rest in Thee."

The great saint states here in few words the origin and interior history of the human race. God made us for Himself—this is the only explanation that satisfies the *heart* of a thinking man, whatever his wild reason may say. Should faulty education and perverse reasoning lead a man to conclude otherwise, there is little that any Christian can do for him. For such a man I have no message.

My appeal is addressed to those who have been previously taught in secret by the wisdom of God. I speak to thirsty hearts whose longings have been wakened by the touch of God within them, and as such they need no reasoned proof. Their restless hearts furnish all the proof they need.

God formed us for Himself. The *Shorter Catechism*, "Agreed upon by the Reverend Assembly of Divines at Westminster," as the old *New England Primer* has it, asks the ancient questions *what* and *why* and answers them in one short sentence hardly matched in any uninspired work. "*Question*: What is the chief end of man? *Answer*: Man's chief end is to glorify God and enjoy Him forever." With this agree the 24 elders who fall on their faces to worship Him that liveth for ever and ever, saying, "Thou art worthy, O Lord, to receive glory and honour and power: for thou hast created all things, and for thy pleasure they are and were created" (Revelation 4:11).

God formed us for His pleasure, and so formed us that we, as well as He, can, in divine communion, enjoy the sweet and mysterious mingling of kindred personalities. He meant us to see Him

> The Lord is very jealous over any saint who is utterly abandoned to Him. He does not let that believer have any pleasures at all outside of Himself.
>
> —Jeanne Guyon

and live with Him and draw our life from His smile. But we have been guilty of that "foul revolt" of which Milton speaks when describing the rebellion of Satan and his hosts. We have broken with God. We have ceased to obey Him or love Him, and in guilt and fear have fled as far as possible from His presence.

*O Thou, in whose presence my soul takes
    delight,
    On whom in affliction I call,
My comfort by day and my song in the
    night,
    My hope, my salvation, my all!*

*Where dost Thou, dear Shepherd, resort
    with Thy sheep,
    To feed them in pastures of love?
Say, why in the valley of death should I
    weep,
    Or alone in this wilderness rove?*

*Dear Shepherd! I hear, and will follow
    Thy call;
    I know the sweet sound of Thy voice;
Restore and defend me, for Thou art my all,
    And in Thee I will ever rejoice.*
                    —Joseph Swain

Yet who can flee from His presence when the heaven and the heaven of heavens cannot contain Him, when as the wisdom of Solomon testifies, the Spirit of the Lord fills the world (see Proverbs 15:3)? The omnipresence of the Lord is one thing, and is a solemn fact necessary to His perfection. The *manifest* Presence is another thing altogether, and from that Presence we have fled, like Adam, to hide among the trees of the garden, or like Peter, to shrink away crying, "Depart from me; for I am a sinful man, O Lord" (Luke 5:8).

And the LORD shall guide thee continually, and satisfy thy soul in drought, and make fat thy bones: and thou shalt be like a watered garden, and like a spring of water, whose waters fail not.

Isaiah 58:11

So the life of man upon the earth is a life away from the Presence, wrenched loose from that "blissful center" which is our right and proper dwelling place, our first estate which we kept not, the loss of which is the cause of our unceasing restlessness.

The whole work of God in redemption is to undo the tragic effects of that foul revolt, and to bring us back again into right and eternal relationship with Himself. This requires that our sins be disposed of satisfactorily, that a full reconciliation be effected and the way opened for us to return again into conscious communion with God and to live again in the Presence as before. Then by His prevenient working within us He moves us to return. This first comes to our notice when our restless hearts feel a yearning for the presence of God and we say within ourselves, "I will arise and go to my Father." That is the first step, and as the Chinese sage Lao-tze has said, "The journey of a thousand miles begins with a first step."

Day 8

Entering the Holy of Holies

For since the beginning of the world men have not heard, nor perceived by the ear, neither hath the eye seen, O God, beside thee, what he hath prepared for him that waiteth for him.

Isaiah 64:4

I will hear what God the LORD will speak: for he will speak peace unto his people, and to his saints.

Psalm 85:8

The interior journey of the soul from the wilds of sin into the enjoyed presence of God is beautifully illustrated in the Old Testament tabernacle. The returning sinner first entered the outer court where he offered a blood sacrifice on the brazen altar and washed himself in the laver that stood near it. Then he passed through a veil into the holy place where no natural light could come, but the golden candlestick which spoke of Jesus, the Light of the

World, threw its soft glow over all. There also was the shewbread to tell of Jesus, the Bread of Life, and the altar of incense, a figure of unceasing prayer.

Though the worshiper had enjoyed so much, still he had not yet entered the presence of God. Another veil separated from the Holy of Holies where above the mercy seat dwelt the very God Himself in awful and glorious manifestation. While the tabernacle stood, only the high priest could enter there, and that but once a year, with blood which he offered for his sins and the sins of the people. It was this last veil which was rent when our Lord gave up the ghost on Calvary, and the sacred writer explains that this rending of the veil opened the way for every worshiper in the world to come by the new and living way straight into the divine Presence.

Everything in the New Testament accords with this Old Testament picture. Ransomed men need no longer pause in fear to enter the Holy of Holies. *God wills that we should push on into His presence and live our whole life there.* This is to be known to us in conscious experience. It is more than a doctrine to be held; it is a life to be enjoyed every moment of every day.

This Flame of the Presence was the beating heart of the Levitical order. Without it all the appointments of the tabernacle were characters of some unknown language, having no meaning for Israel or for us. The greatest fact of the tabernacle was that *Jehovah was there*; a Presence was waiting within the veil.

Take time to be separate from all friends and all duties, all cares and all joys; time to be still and quiet before God. Take time not only to secure stillness from man and the world, but from self and its energy. Let the Word and prayer be very precious; but re-member, even these may hinder the quiet waiting. The activity of the mind in study-ing the Word, or giving expression to its thoughts in prayer, the activities of the heart, with its desires and hopes and fears, may so engage us that we do not come to the still waiting on the All-Glorious One. Though at first it may appear difficult to know how thus quietly to wait, with the ac-tivities of mind and heart for a time sub-dued, every effort after it will be rewarded; we shall find that it grows upon us, and the little season of silent worship will bring a peace and a rest that give a blessing not only in prayer, but all the day.
—Andrew Murray

Similarly, the presence of God is the central fact of Christianity. At the heart of the Christian message is God Himself waiting for His redeemed children to push in to conscious awareness of His presence. That type of Christianity which happens now to be the vogue knows this Presence only in theory. It fails to stress the Christian's privilege of present realization. According to its teachings we are in the presence of God positionally, and nothing is said about the need to experience that Presence actually. The fiery urge that drove men like McCheyne is wholly missing. And the present generation of Christians measures itself by this imperfect rule. Ignoble contentment

There is something exceedingly improving to the mind in a contemplation of the Divinity. It is a subject so vast, that all our thoughts are lost in its immensity; so deep, that our pride is drowned in its infinity. Other subjects we can compass and grapple with; in them we feel a kind of self-content and go our way with the thought, "Behold, I am wise." But when we come to this master-science, finding that our plumb line cannot sound its depth, and that our eagle eye cannot see its height, we turn away with the thought, "I am but of yesterday, and know nothing." No subject of contemplation will tend more to humble the mind than thoughts of God.

—Charles H. Spurgeon

takes the place of burning zeal. We are satisfied to rest in our *judicial* possessions and, for the most part, we bother ourselves very little about the absence of personal experience.

Who is this within the veil who dwells in fiery manifestations? It is none other than God Himself. "One God, the Father Almighty, Maker of heaven and earth, and of all things visible and invisible." It is "one Lord Jesus Christ, the only begotten Son of God; begotten of His Father before all worlds, God of God, Light of Light, Very God of Very God; begotten, not made; being of one substance with the Father." And it is "the Holy Ghost, the Lord and Giver of life, Who proceedeth from the Father and the Son, Who with the Father and the Son together is worshiped and glorified." Yet this holy Trinity is one God, for "we worship one God in Trinity, and Trinity in Unity; neither confounding the Persons, nor dividing the Substance. For there is one Person of the Father, another of the Son, and another of the Holy Ghost. But the Godhead of the Father, of the Son, and of the Holy Ghost, is all one: the glory equal and the majesty co-eternal." So in part

> *God hides nothing. His very work from the beginning is revelation—a casting aside of veil after veil, a showing unto men of truth after truth.*
>
> *— George MacDonald*

run the ancient creeds, and so the inspired Word declares.

Behind the veil is God, that God after whom the world, with strange inconsistency, has felt, "if haply they might . . . find him" (Acts 17:27). He has discovered Himself to some extent in nature, but more perfectly in the Incarnation. Now He waits to show Himself in ravishing fullness to the humble of soul and the pure in heart.

> *Here, O my Lord, I see Thee face to face;*
>   *Here would I touch and handle things*
>   *unseen;*
> *Here, grasp with firmer hand eternal grace,*
>   *And all my weariness upon Thee lean.*
>
> *I have no help but Thine, nor do I need*
>   *Another arm save Thine to lean upon;*
> *It is enough, my Lord, enough indeed;*
>   *My strength is in Thy might, Thy might*
>   *alone.*
>
> —Horatius Bonar

Day 9

The Wonder of God's Presence

O LORD, I know that the way of man is not
in himself: it is not in man that walketh to
direct his steps.

Jeremiah 10:23

For this God is our God for ever and ever:
he will be our guide even unto death.

Psalm 48:14

The world is perishing for lack of the knowledge
of God, and the Church is famishing for want of
His presence. The instant cure of most of our religious ills would be to enter the Presence in spiritual
experience, to become suddenly aware that we are in
God and God is in us. This would lift us out of our
pitiful narrowness and cause our hearts to be en-
larged. This would burn away the impurities from
our lives as the bugs and fungi
were burned away by the fire that
dwelt in the bush.

What a broad world to roam
in, what a sea to swim in is this
God and Father of our Lord Jesus

Christ. He is *eternal*. He antedates time and is wholly independent of it. Time began in Him and will end in Him. To it He pays no tribute and from it He suffers no change.

He is *immutable*. He has never changed and can never change in any smallest measure. To change He would need to go from better to worse or from worse to better. He cannot do either, for being perfect He cannot become more perfect, and if He were to become less perfect He would be less than God.

He is *omniscient*. He knows in one free and effortless act all matter, all spirit, all relationships, all events. He has no past and He has no future. He *is*, and none of the limiting and qualifying terms used of creatures can apply to Him.

Love and *mercy* and *righteousness* are His, and *holiness* so ineffable that no comparisons or figures will avail to express it. Only fire can give even a remote conception of it. In fire He appeared at the burning bush; in the pillar of fire He dwelt through all the long wilderness journey. The fire that glowed between the wings of the cherubim in the holy place was called the Shekinah, the Presence, through the years of Israel's glory, and when the Old had given place to the New, He came at Pentecost as a fiery flame and rested upon each disciple.

Spinoza wrote of the intellectual love of God, and he had a measure of truth there. But the highest love of God is not intellectual, it is spiritual.

God is spirit and only the spirit of a man can know Him really. In the deep spirit of a man the fire must glow or his love is not the true love of God. The great of the kingdom have been those who loved God more than others did. We all know who they have been and gladly pay tribute to the depth and sincerity of their devotion. We have but to pause for a moment and their names come trooping past us, smelling of myrrh and aloes and cassia out of the ivory palaces.

Frederick Faber was one whose soul panted after God as the roe pants after the water brook, and the measure in which God revealed Himself to his seeking heart set the good man's whole life afire with a burning adoration rivaling that of the seraphim before the throne. His love for God extended to the three Persons of the Godhead equally, yet he seemed to feel for each One a special kind of love reserved for Him alone. Of God the Father he sings:

> *A man's spiritual health is exactly proportional to his love for God.*
>
> —C.S. Lewis

Only to sit and think of God
 Oh what a joy it is!
To think the thought, to breathe the Name;
 Earth has no higher bliss.

Father of Jesus, love's reward!
 What rapture it will be,

Prostrate before Thy throne to lie,
　　And gaze and gaze on Thee!

His love for the Person of Christ was so intense that it threatened to consume him. It burned within him as a sweet and holy madness and flowed from his lips like molten gold. In one of his sermons he says,

> Wherever we turn in the church of God, there is Jesus. He is the beginning, middle and end of everything to us. . . . There is nothing good, nothing holy, nothing beautiful, nothing joyous which He is not to His servants. No one need to be poor, because, if he chooses, he can have Jesus for his own property and possession. No one need be downcast, for Jesus is the joy of heaven, and it is His joy to enter into sorrowful hearts. We can exaggerate about many

O God, thou art my God; early will I seek thee: my soul thirsteth for thee, my flesh longeth for thee in a dry and thirsty land, where no water is;

Because thy lovingkindness is better than life, my lips shall praise thee.

Thus will I bless thee while I live: I will lift up my hands in thy name.

My soul shall be satisfied as with marrow and fatness; and my mouth shall praise thee with joyful lips.

Psalm 63:1, 3-5

things; but we can never exaggerate our obligation to Jesus or the compassionate abundance of the love of Jesus to us. All our lives long we might talk of Jesus, and yet we should never come to an end of the sweet things that might be said of Him. Eternity will not be long enough to learn all He is, or to praise Him for all He has done, but then, that matters not; for we shall be always with Him, and we desire nothing more.

I have no home, until I am in the realized presence of God. This holy presence is my inward home, and, until I experience it, I am a homeless wanderer, a straying sheep in a waste howling wilderness.

—Anonymous, 1841

And addressing our Lord directly he says to Him:

I love Thee so, I know not how
    My transports to control;
Thy love is like a burning fire
    Within my very soul.

Faber's blazing love extended also to the Holy Spirit. Not only in his theology did he acknowledge His deity and full equality with the Father and the Son, but he celebrated it constantly in his songs and in his prayers. He literally pressed his forehead to the ground in his eager, fervid worship of the Third Person of the Godhead. In one of his great hymns to the Holy Spirit he sums up his burning devotion thus:

O Spirit, beautiful and dread!
My heart is fit to break
With love of all Thy tenderness
For us poor sinners' sake.

I have risked the tedium of quotation that I might show by pointed example what I have set out to say, viz., that God is so vastly wonderful, so utterly and completely delightful that He can, without anything other than Himself, meet and overflow the deepest demands of our total nature, mysterious and deep as that nature is. Such worship as Faber knew (and he is but one of a great company which no man can number) can never come from a mere doctrinal knowledge of God. Hearts that are "fit to break" with love for the Godhead are those who have been in the Presence and have looked with opened eye upon the majesty of Deity. Men of the breaking hearts had a quality about them not known to nor understood by common men. They habitually spoke with spiritual authority. They had been in the presence of God and they reported what they saw there. They were prophets, not scribes, for the scribe tells us what he has read, and the prophet tells what he has seen.

The distinction is not an imaginary one. Between the scribe who has read and the prophet who has seen there is a difference as wide as the sea. We are overrun today with orthodox scribes, but the prophets, where are they? The hard voice of the scribe sounds over evangelicalism, but the Church waits for the tender voice of the saint who has penetrated the veil and has gazed with inward eye upon the wonder that is God. And yet, thus to penetrate, to push in sensitive living experience into the holy Presence, is a privilege open to every child of God.

Breathe on me, Breath of God,
  Fill me with life anew,
That I may love what Thou dost love,
  And do what Thou wouldst do.

Breathe on me, Breath of God,
  Until my heart is pure,
Until with Thee I will one will
  To do or to endure.

Breathe on me, Breath of God,
  Till I am wholly Thine,
Till all this earthly part of me
  Glows with Thy fire divine.
      —Edwin Hatch

~Only to Sit and Think of God . . .~

— Frederick W. Faber

God is not affected by our mutability; our changes do not alter Him. When we are restless, He remains serene and calm; when we are low, selfish, mean, or dispirited, He is still the unalterable I Am.
— Frederick W. Robertson

Even here and now, whenever the heart begins to burn with a desire for God, she is made able to receive the uncreated light and, inspired and fulfilled by the gifts of the Holy Ghost, she tastes the joys of heaven. She transcends all visible things and is raised to the sweetness of eternal life. Herein truly is perfect love; when all the intent of the mind, all the secret working of the heart, is lifted up into the love of God.
— Richard Rolle of Hampole

God works powerfully, but for the most part gently and gradually.
— John Newton

Day 10

Removing the Self-Life Veil

*One thing alone, dear Lord, I dread
    To have a secret spot
That separates my soul from Thee,
    And yet to know it not.*
                    —Frederick Faber

*W*ith the veil removed by the rending of Jesus' flesh, with nothing on God's side to prevent us from entering, why do we tarry without? Why do we consent to abide all our days just outside the Holy of Holies and never enter at all to look upon God? We hear the Bridegroom say, "let me see thy countenance, let me hear thy voice; for sweet is thy voice, and thy countenance is comely" (Song of Songs 2:14). We sense that the call is for us, but still we fail to draw near, and the years pass and we grow old and tired in the outer courts of the tabernacle. What hinders us?

The answer usually given, simply that we are "cold," will not explain all the facts. There is something more serious than coldness of heart, something that may be back of that coldness and be the cause of its existence. What is it? What but the presence of *a veil in our hearts*? A veil not taken away as the first veil was, but which remains there still shutting out the light and hiding the face of God from us. It is the veil of our fleshly, fallen nature living on, unjudged within us, uncrucified and unrepudiated. It is the close-woven veil of the self-life which we have never truly acknowledged, of which we have been secretly ashamed, and which for these reasons we have never brought to the judgment of the cross. It is not too mysterious, this opaque veil, nor is it hard to identify. We have but to look into our own hearts and we shall see it there, sewn and patched and repaired it may be, but there nevertheless, an enemy to our lives and an effective block to our spiritual progress.

God is too wise not to know all about us, and what is really best for us. He is too good not to desire our highest good. If what He has appointed for us does not seem to us the best, or even to be good, we need to remember that He sees further than we do, and that we shall understand Him in time when His plans have unfolded themselves.

— Henry Parry Liddon

This veil is not a beautiful thing and it is not a thing about which we commonly care to talk. But I am addressing the thirsting souls who are determined to follow God, and I know they will not turn back because the way leads temporarily through the blackened hills. The urge of God within them will assure their continuing pursuit. They will face the facts, however unpleasant, and endure the cross for the joy set before them. So I am bold to name the threads out of which this inner veil is woven.

It is woven of the fine threads of the self-life, the hyphenated sins of the human spirit. They are not something we *do*, they are something we *are*, and therein lies both their subtlety and their power.

To be specific, the self-sins are self-righteousness, self-pity, self-confidence, self-sufficiency, self-admiration, self-love and a host of others like them. They dwell too deep within us and are too much a part of our natures to come to our attention till the light of God is focused upon them. The grosser manifestations of these sins—egotism, exhibitionism, self-promotion—are strangely tolerated in Christian leaders, even in circles of impeccable orthodoxy. They are so much in evidence as actually, for many people, to become identified with the gospel. I trust it is not a cynical observation to say that they appear these days to be a requisite for popularity in some sections of the church visible. Promoting self under the guise of promoting Christ is currently so common as to excite little notice.

One should suppose that proper instruction in the doctrines of man's depravity and the necessity for justification through the righteousness of Christ alone would deliver us from the power of the self-sins, but it does not work that way. Self can live unrebuked at the very altar. It can watch the bleeding Victim die and not be in the least affected by what it sees. It can fight for the faith of the reformers and preach eloquently the creed of salvation by grace and gain strength by its efforts. To tell the truth, it seems actually to feed upon orthodoxy and is more at home in a Bible conference than in a tavern. Our very state of longing after God may afford it an excellent condition under which to thrive and grow.

God delivers us from sin; we have to deliver ourselves from individuality, that is, to present our natural life to God and sacrifice it until it is transformed into a spiritual life by obedience.

—D.W. Lambert

Self is the opaque veil that hides the face of God from us. It can be removed only in spiritual experience, never by mere instruction. We may as well try to instruct leprosy out of our system. There must be a work of God in destruction before we are free. We must invite the cross to do its deadly work within us. We must bring our self-sins to the cross for judgment. We must prepare ourselves for an ordeal of suffering in some measure like that through which our Savior passed when He suffered under Pontius Pilate.

Let us remember that when we talk of the rending of the veil we are speaking in a figure, and the thought of it is poetical, almost pleasant, but in actuality there is nothing pleasant about it. In human experience that veil is made of living spiritual tissue; it is composed of the sentient, quivering stuff of which our whole beings consist, and to touch it is to touch us where we feel pain. To tear it away is to injure us, to hurt us and make us bleed. To say otherwise is to make the cross no cross and death no death at all. It is never fun to die. To rip through the dear and tender stuff of which life is made can never be anything but deeply painful. Yet that is what the cross did to Jesus, and it is what the cross would do to every man to set him free.

> God gives us the cross,
> and then the cross gives us God.
> —Jeanne Guyon

Let us beware of tinkering with our inner life, hoping ourselves to rend the veil. God must do everything for us. Our part is to yield and trust. We must confess, forsake, repudiate the self-life and then reckon it crucified. But we must be careful to distinguish lazy "acceptance" from the real work of God. We must insist upon the work being done. We dare not rest content with a neat doctrine of self-crucifixion. That is to imitate Saul and spare the best of the sheep and the oxen.

Insist that the work be done in very truth and it will be done. The cross is rough and it is deadly, but it is effective. It does not keep its victim hanging there forever. There comes a moment when its work is finished and the suffering victim dies. After that is resurrection glory and power, and the pain is forgotten for joy that the veil is taken away and we have entered in actual spiritual experience the presence of the living God.

> *Lord, how excellent are Thy ways, and how devious and dark are the ways of man. Show us how to die, that we may rise again to newness of life. Rend the veil of our self-life from the top down as Thou didst rend the veil of the temple. We would draw near in full assurance of faith. We would dwell with Thee in daily experience here on this earth so that we may be accustomed to the glory when we enter Thy heaven to dwell with Thee there. In Jesus' name. Amen.*

~The Weed of Self~

*Self is one of the toughest plants that
grows in the garden of life. It is, in fact, in-
destructible by any human means. Just
when we are sure it is dead, it turns up
somewhere as robust as ever to trouble our
peace and poison the fruit of our lives.*
— AWT in
Man: The Dwelling Place of God

A man's self is his greatest cross.
— Francois Fenélon

*What other dungeon is so dark
as one's own heart! What jailer so
inexorable as one's self!*
— Nathaniel Hawthorne

Self-praise is no recommendation.
— Latin Proverb

*Self-love is a medium of a peculiar kind; it
magnifies everything that is amiss in others
at the same time that it lessens everything
that is amiss in ourselves.*
— Bishop Joseph Butler

A proud man is always looking down on things and people; and, of course, as long as you're looking down, you can't see something that's above you.

— C.S. Lewis

When in His mercy God leads a soul in the higher paths of sanctification, He begins by stripping it of all self-confidence, and to this end He allows our own schemes to fail, our judgment to mislead us. We grope and totter and make countless mistakes until we learn to mistrust ourselves and to put all our confidence in Him.

—Jean Nicholas Grou

It is the great moment of our lives when we decide that sin must die right out, not be curbed or suppressed or counteracted, but crucified.

— Oswald Chambers

Day 11

The Waiting God

O taste and see that the LORD is good:
blessed is the man that trusteth in him. O
fear the LORD, ye his saints: for there is no
want to them that fear him. The young li-
ons do lack, and suffer hunger: but they
that seek the LORD shall not want any good
thing.

Psalm 34:8-10

*C*anon Holmes, of India, more than 25 years ago
called attention to the inferential character of the
average man's faith in God. To most people God is
an inference, not a reality. He is a deduction from
evidence which they consider adequate, but He remains personally unknown to the individual. "He
must be," they say, "therefore we believe He is."
Others do not go even so far as this; they know of
Him only by hearsay. They have
never bothered to think the matter
out for themselves, but have heard
about Him from others, and have
put belief in Him into the back of
their minds along with various

odds and ends that make up their total creed. To many others, God is but an ideal, another name for goodness or beauty or truth; or He is law or life or the creative impulse back of the phenomena of existence.

These notions about God are many and varied, but they who hold them have one thing in common: They do not know God in personal experience. The possibility of intimate acquaintance with Him has not entered their minds. While admitting His existence they do not think of Him as being knowable in the sense that we know things or people.

Christians, to be sure, go further than this, at least in theory. Their creed requires them to believe in the personality of God, and they have been taught to pray, "Our Father which art in heaven" (Luke 11:2). Now personality and fatherhood carry with them the idea of the possibility of personal acquaintance. This is admitted, I say, in theory, but for millions of Christians, nevertheless, God is no more real than He is to the non-Christian. They go through life trying to love an ideal and be loyal to a mere principle.

God's limitless knowledge and perfect wisdom enable Him to work rationally beyond the bounds of our rational knowing. For this

reason we cannot predict God's actions as we can predict the movements of the heavenly bodies, so He constantly astonishes us as He moves in freedom through His universe. So imperfectly do we know Him that it may be said that one invariable concomitant of a true encounter with God is delighted wonder. No matter how high our expectation may be, when God finally moves into the field of our spiritual awareness we are sure to be astonished by His power to overwhelm the mind and fascinate the soul.
—*AWT in* That Incredible Christian

◊   ◊   ◊

Over against all this cloudy vagueness stands the clear scriptural doctrine that God can be known in personal experience. A loving Personality dominates the Bible, walking among the trees of the garden and breathing fragrance over every scene. Always a living Person is present, speaking, pleading, loving, working and manifesting Himself whenever and wherever His people have the receptivity necessary to receive the manifestation.

The Bible assumes as a self-evident fact that men can know God with at least the same degree of immediacy as they know any other person or thing that comes within the field of their experience. The same terms are used to express the knowledge of

God as are used to express knowledge of physical things. "O *taste* and see that the LORD is good" (Psalm 34:8). "All thy garments *smell* of myrrh, and aloes, and cassia, out of the ivory palaces" (45:8). "My sheep *hear* my voice" (John 10:27). "Blessed are the pure in heart: for they shall *see* God" (Matthew 5:8). These are but four of countless such passages from the Word of God. And more important than any proof text is the fact that the whole import of Scripture is toward this belief.

What can all this mean except that we have in our hearts organs by means of which we can know God as certainly as we know material things through our familiar five senses? We apprehend the physical world by exercising the faculties given us for that purpose, and we possess spiritual faculties by means of which we can know God and the spiritual world if we will obey the Spirit's urge and begin to use them.

That a saving work must first be done in the heart is taken for granted here. The spiritual faculties of the unregenerate man lie asleep in his nature, unused, and for every purpose dead. That is

> *Christian faith is a grand cathedral, with divinely pictured windows. Standing without, you see no glory, nor can imagine any. But standing within, every ray of light reveals a harmony of unspeakable splendors.*
>
> —Nathaniel Hawthorne

the stroke which has fallen upon us by sin. They may be quickened to active life again by the operation of the Holy Spirit in regeneration. That is one of the immeasurable benefits which comes to us through Christ's atoning work on the cross.

But why do the very ransomed children of God themselves know so little of that habitual, conscious communion with God which Scripture offers? The answer is because of our chronic unbelief. Faith enables our spiritual sense to function. Where faith is defective the result will be inward insensibility and numbness toward spiritual things. This is the condition of vast numbers of Christians today. No proof is necessary to support that statement. We have but to converse with the first Christian we meet or enter the first church we open to acquire all the proof we need.

> *Every man will have to decide for himself whether or not he can afford the terrible luxury of unbelief.*
>
> —AWT in That Incredible Christian

A spiritual kingdom lies all about us, enclosing us, embracing us, altogether within reach of our inner selves, waiting for us to recognize it. God Himself is here awaiting our response to His presence. This eternal world will come alive to us the moment we begin to reckon upon its reality.

Oh, for a closer walk with God,
A calm and heavenly frame,
A light to shine upon the road
That leads me to the Lamb!

Where is the blessedness I knew,
When first I saw the Lord?
Where is the soul-refreshing view
Of Jesus and His Word?

What peaceful hours I once enjoyed!
How sweet their memory still!
But they have left an aching void
The world can never fill.
                    —William Cowper

◇   ◇   ◇

Day 12

The Reality of God

Reality is not only more fantastic than we think, but also much more fantastic than we imagine.

—J.B.S. Haldane

J have used two words which I must at least make clear what I mean when I use them. They are *reckon* and *reality*.

What do I mean by *reality*? I mean that which has existence apart from any idea any mind may have of it, and which would exist if there were no mind anywhere to entertain a thought of it. That which is real has being in itself. It does not depend upon the observer for its validity.

I am aware that there are those who love to poke fun at the plain man's idea of reality. They are the idealists who spin endless proofs that nothing is real outside of the mind. They are the relativists who like to show that there are no fixed points in the universe from which we can measure anything.

They smile down upon us from their lofty intellectual peaks and settle us to their own satisfaction by fastening upon us the reproachful term *absolutist*. The Christian is not put out of countenance by this show of contempt. He can smile right back at them, for he knows that there is only One who is absolute, that is God. But he knows also that the Absolute One has made this world for man's use, and while there is nothing fixed or real in the last meaning of the words (the meaning as applied to God), *for every purpose of human life we are permitted to act as if there were*. And every man does act thus except the mentally sick. These unfortunates also have trouble with reality, but they are consistent; they insist upon living in accordance with their ideas of things. They are honest, and it is their very honesty which constitutes them a social problem.

The idealists and relativists

Why doesn't the sky fall down? Why is it that stars and planets do not go tearing apart and ripping off into chaos? Because there is a Presence that makes all things consist—and it is the Presence of that One who upholdeth all things by the word of His power. This is basically a spiritual explanation, for this universe can only be explained by spiritual and eternal laws.

—AWT in **Who Put Jesus on the Cross?**

are not mentally sick. They prove their soundness by living their lives according to the very notions of reality which they in theory repudiate and by counting upon the very fixed points which they prove are not there. They could earn a lot more respect for their notions if they were willing to live by them; but this they are careful not to do. Their ideas are brain-deep, not life-deep. Wherever life touches them they repudiate their theories and live like other men.

Reality, in fact, is always something you couldn't have guessed. That's one of the reasons I believe Christianity. It has just that queer twist about it that real things have.
—C.S. Lewis

The Christian is too sincere to play with ideas for their own sake. He takes no pleasure in the mere spinning of gossamer webs for display. All his beliefs are practical. They are geared into his life. By them he lives or dies, stands or falls for this world and for all time to come. From the insincere man he turns away.

The sincere, plain man knows that the world is real. He finds it here when he wakes to consciousness, and he knows that he did not think it into being. It was here waiting for him when he came, and he knows that when he prepares to leave this earthly scene it will be here still to bid him good-bye as he departs. By the deep wisdom of life he is wiser than a thousand men who doubt. He stands upon the earth and feels the wind and rain in his face, and he knows that they are real. He sees the sun by day and the stars by night. He sees the hot lightning play out of the dark thundercloud. He hears the sounds of nature and the cries of human joy and pain. These he knows are real. He lies down on the cool earth at night and has no fear that it will prove illusory or fail him while he sleeps. In the morning the firm ground will be under him, the blue sky above him and the rocks and trees around him as when he closed his eyes the night before. So he lives and rejoices in a world of reality.

Many, O LORD my God, are thy wonderful works which thou hast done, and thy thoughts which are to us-ward: they cannot be reckoned up in order unto thee: if I would declare and speak of them, they are more than can be numbered.

Psalm 40:5

With his five senses he engages this real world. All things necessary to his physical existence he apprehends by the faculties with which he has been equipped by the God who created him and placed him in such a world as this.

Now by our definition also God is real. He is real in the absolute and final sense that nothing else is. All other reality is contingent upon His. The great reality is God, the Author of that lower and dependent reality which makes up the sum of created things, including ourselves. God has objective existence independent of and apart from any notions which we may have concerning Him. The worshiping heart does not create its Object. It finds Him here when it wakes from its moral slumber in the morning of its regeneration.

Another word that must be cleared up is *reckon*. This does not mean to visualize or imagine. Imagination is not faith. The two are not only different from, but stand in sharp opposition to each other. Imagination projects unreal images out of the mind and seeks to attach reality to them. Faith creates nothing; it simply reckons upon that which is already *there*.

God and the spiritual world are real. We can reckon upon them with as much assurance as we reckon upon the familiar world around us. Spiritual things are there (or rather we should say *here*) inviting our attention and challenging our trust.

◇   ◇   ◇

Oh, for a faith that will not shrink,
   Though pressed by many a foe,
That will not tremble on the brink
   Of any earthly woe!

That bears, unmoved, the world's dread
      frown,
   Nor heeds its scornful smile;
That seas of trouble cannot drown,
   Nor Satan's arts beguile.

Lord, give us such a faith as this,
   And then, whate'er may come,
We'll taste, e'en here, the hallowed bliss
   Of an eternal home.
                    —William H. Bathurst

◇   ◇   ◇

~Faith . . . A Form of Knowledge which Transcends the Intellect~

— Malcolm Muggeridge

Now faith is the substance of things hoped for, the evidence of things not seen. . . . But without faith it is impossible to please him; for he that cometh to God must believe that he is, and that he is a rewarder of them that diligently seek him.

They that trust in the LORD shall be as mount Zion, which cannot be removed, but abideth for ever.

Thou wilt keep him in perfect peace, whose mind is stayed on thee: because he trusteth in thee.

Hebrews 11:1, 6; Psalm 125:1; Isaiah 26:3

We must have faith, and let us not apologize for it, for faith is an organ of knowledge and can tell us more about ultimate reality than all the findings of science. We are not opposed to science, but we recognize its proper limitations and refuse to stop where it is compelled to stop. The Bible tells of another world too fine for the instruments of scientific research to discover. By faith we engage that world and make it ours. It is accessible to us through the blood of the everlasting covenant. If we will believe we may even now enjoy the presence of God and the ministry of His heavenly messengers. Only unbelief can rob us of this royal privilege.

— AWT in Of God and Men

Nothing can take the place of the touch of God in the soul and the sense of Someone there.

—AWT in The Divine Conquest

It takes real faith to begin to live the life of heaven while still upon the earth, for this requires that we rise above the law of moral gravitation and bring to our everyday living the high wisdom of God. And since this wisdom is contrary to that of the world, conflict is bound to result. This, however, is a small price to pay for the inestimable privilege of following Christ.

—AWT in Born After Midnight

Day 13

The Unseen God

*A thousand voices clamor for our attention,
and a thousand causes vie for our support.
But until we have learned to be satisfied
with fellowship with God, until He is our
rock and our fortress, we will be restless
with our place in the world.*

— *Erwin W. Lutzer*

*O*ur trouble is that we have established bad thought habits. We habitually think of the visible world as real and doubt the reality of any other. We do not deny the existence of the spiritual world but we doubt that it is real in the accepted meaning of the word.

The world of sense intrudes upon our attention day and night for the whole of our lifetime. It is clamorous, insistent and self-demonstrating. It does not appeal to our faith; it is here, assaulting our five senses, demanding to be accepted as real and final. But sin has so clouded the lenses of our hearts that we cannot see that other reality, the

City of God, shining around us. The world of sense triumphs. The visible becomes the enemy of the invisible, the temporal, of the eternal. That is the curse inherited by every member of Adam's tragic race.

At the root of the Christian life lies belief in the invisible. The object of the Christians's faith is unseen reality.

Our uncorrected thinking, influenced by the blindness of our natural hearts and the intrusive ubiquity of visible things, tends to draw a contrast between the spiritual and the real—but actually no such contrast exists. The antithesis lies elsewhere—between the real and the imaginary, between the spiritual and the material, between the temporal and the eternal; but between the spiritual and the real, never. The spiritual is real.

> To be "spiritually minded" simply means to look at earth from heaven's point of view. The spiritually minded believer makes his decisions on the basis of eternal values and not the passing fads of society.
>
> —Warren Wiersbe

If we would rise into that region of light and power plainly beckoning us through the Scriptures of truth, we must break the evil habit of ignoring the spiritual. We must shift our interest from the seen to the unseen. For the great unseen Reality is God. "He that cometh to God must believe that he is, and that he is a rewarder of them that diligently seek him" (Hebrews 11:6). This is basic in the life of faith. From there we can rise to unlimited heights. "Ye believe in God," said our Lord Jesus Christ, "believe also in me" (John 14:1). Without the first there can be no second.

If we truly want to follow God, we must seek to be other-worldly. This I say knowing well that word has been used with scorn by the sons of this world and applied to the Christian as a badge of reproach. So be it. Every man must choose his world. If we who follow Christ, with all the facts before us and knowing what we are about, deliberately choose the kingdom of God as our sphere of interest, I see no reason why anyone should object. If we lose by it, the loss is our own; if we gain, we rob no one by so doing. The "other world," which is the object of this world's disdain and the subject of the drunkard's mocking song, is our carefully chosen goal and the object of our holiest longing.

But we must avoid the common fault of pushing the "other world" into the future. It is not future, but present. It parallels our familiar physical world, and the doors between the two worlds are open. "Ye are come," says the writer to the Hebrews (and the tense is plainly present), "unto mount Zion, and unto the city of the living God, the heavenly Jerusalem, and to an innumerable company of angels, to the general assembly and church of the firstborn, which are written in heaven, and to God the Judge of all, and to the spirits of just men made perfect, and to Jesus the mediator of the new covenant, and to the blood of sprinkling, that speaketh better things than that of Abel" (Hebrews 12:22–24). All these things are contrasted with "the mount that might be touched" (12:18) and "the sound of a trumpet, and the voice of words" (12:19) that might be heard. May we not safely conclude that, as the realities of Mount Sinai were apprehended by the senses, so the realities of Mount Zion are to be grasped by the soul? And this not by any trick of the imagination but in downright actuality. The soul has eyes with which to see and ears with which to hear. Feeble they may be from long disuse, but by the life-giving touch of Christ they are now alive and capable of sharpest sight and most sensitive hearing.

How far away is heaven? It is not so far as some imagine. It wasn't very far away from Daniel. It was not so far off that Elijah's prayer and those of others could not be heard there. Men full of the Spirit can look right in to heaven.

—Dwight L. Moody

◇　◇　◇

Aim at heaven and you get earth thrown in.
Aim at earth and you get neither.
—C.S. Lewis

◇　◇　◇

As we begin to focus upon God, the things of the Spirit will take shape before our inner eyes. Obedience to the word of Christ will bring an inward revelation of the Godhead (John 14:21–23). It will give acute perception enabling us to see God even as is promised to the pure in heart. A new God-consciousness will seize upon us and we shall begin to taste and hear and inwardly feel God, who is our life and our all. There will be seen the constant shining of "the true Light, which lighteth every man that cometh into the world" (John 1:9). More and more, as our faculties grow sharper and more sure, God will become to us the great All, and His presence the glory and wonder of our lives.

O God, quicken to life every power within me, that I may lay hold on eternal things. Open my eyes that I may see; give me acute spiritual perception; enable me to taste Thee and know that Thou art good. Make heaven more real to me than any earthly thing has ever been. Amen.

Day 14

The Universal God

God is over all things, under all things, outside all; within, but not enclosed; without, but not excluded; above, but not raised up; below, but not depressed; wholly above, presiding; wholly without, embracing; wholly within, filling.

—Hildebert of Lavardin

*I*n all Christian teaching certain basic truths are found, hidden at times, and rather assumed than asserted, but necessary to all truth as the primary colors are found in and necessary to the finished painting. Such a truth is the divine immanence.

God dwells in His creation and is everywhere indivisibly present in all His works. This is boldly taught by prophet and apostle, and is accepted by Christian theology generally. That is, it appears in the books, but for some reason it has not sunk into the average Christian's heart so as to become a part of his believing self. Christian teachers shy away from its full implications and, if they mention it at all, mute it down till it has little meaning. I would guess the reason for this to be the fear of being charged with pantheism. But the doctrine of the divine Presence is definitely not pantheism.

Pantheism's error is too palpable to deceive anyone. It is that God is the sum of all created things. Nature and God are one, so that whoever touches a leaf or a stone touches God. That is, of course, to degrade the glory of the incorruptible Deity and, in an effort to make all things divine, banish all divinity from the world entirely.

> Do you not know that your great sin is this: the all-pervading and eternal Presence is here, and you cannot feel Him?
>
> —A.W. Tozer in Who Put Jesus on the Cross?

The truth is that while God dwells in His world He is separated from it by a gulf forever impassable. However closely He may be identified with the work of His hands, they are and must eternally be other than He, and He is and must be antecedent to and independent of them. He is transcendent above all His works even while He is immanent within them.

What does the divine immanence mean in direct Christian experience? It means simply that *God is here.* Wherever we are, God is here. There is no place, there can be no place, where He is not. Ten million intelligences standing at as many points in space and separated by incomprehensible distances can each one say with equal truth, God is here. No point is nearer to God than any other point. It is exactly as near to God from any place as it is from any other place. No one is in mere distance any further from or any nearer to God than any other person.

> *God is an infinite circle whose center is everywhere and whose circumference is nowhere.*
>
> *—Saint Augustine of Hippo*

◇   ◇   ◇

*God is altogether present wherever
He is present at all.*
—AWT in
The Divine Conquest

◇   ◇   ◇

These are truths believed by every instructed Christian. It remains for us to think on them and pray over them until they begin to glow within us.

~How to Enjoy the Presence of God~

1. The most holy and necessary practice in our spiritual life is the presence of God. That means finding constant pleasure in His divine company, speaking humbly and lovingly with Him in all seasons, at every moment, without limiting the conversation in any way. This is especially important in times of temptation, sorrow, separation from God, and even in times of unfaithfulness and sin.

2. We must try to converse with God in little ways while we do our work; not in memorized prayer, not trying to recite previously formed thoughts. Rather, we should purely and simply reveal our hearts as the words come to us.

3. We must do everything with great care, avoiding impetuous actions, which are evidence of a disordered spirit. God wishes us to work gently, calmly, and lovingly with Him, asking Him to accept our work. By this continual attention to God, we will "resist the devil and cause him to flee" (James 4:7).

4. Whatever we do, even if we are reading the Word or praying, we should stop for a few minutes—as often as possible—to praise God from the depths of our hearts, to enjoy Him there in secret. Since you believe that God is always with you, no matter what you may be doing, why shouldn't you stop for awhile to adore Him, to praise Him, to petition Him, to offer Him your heart, and to thank Him?

— Brother Lawrence in
The Practice of the Presence of God

Day 15

The All-Pervading God

Begin where we will, God is there first.
—AWT in The Divine Conquest

*I*n the beginning *God* . . ." (Genesis 1:1). Not *matter*, for matter is not self-causing. It requires an antecedent cause, and God is that Cause. Not *law*, for law is but a name for the course which all creation follows. That course had to be planned, and the Planner is God. Not *mind*, for mind also is a created thing and must have a Creator back of it. In the beginning *God*, the uncaused Cause of matter, mind and law. There we must begin.

Adam sinned and, in his panic, frantically tried to do the impossible; he tried to hide from the presence of God. David also must have had wild thoughts of trying to escape from the Presence, for he wrote, "Whither shall I go from thy spirit? or whither shall I flee from thy presence?" (Psalm 139:7). Then he proceeded through one of his most beautiful psalms to celebrate the glory of the divine immanence. "If I ascend up into heaven, thou art

91

there: if I make my bed in hell, behold, thou art there. If I take the wings of the morning, and dwell in the uttermost parts of the sea; even there shall thy hand lead me, and thy right hand shall hold me" (139:8–10). And he knew that God's *being* and God's *seeing* are the same, that the seeing Presence had been with him even before he was born, watching the mystery of unfolding life. Solomon exclaimed, "But will God indeed dwell on the earth? behold, the heaven and the heaven of heav-

> A philosopher once asked, "Where is God?" The Christian answered, "Let me first ask you— where is He not?"

ens cannot contain thee; how much less this house that I have builded" (1 Kings 8:27). Paul assured the Athenians that "he be not far from every one of us: for in him we live, and move, and have our being" (Acts 17:27–28).

If God is present at every point in space, if we cannot go where He is not, cannot even conceive of a place where He is not, why then has not that Presence become the one universally celebrated fact of the world? The patriarch Jacob, "in the waste howling wilderness" (Deuteronomy 32:10), gave the answer to that question. He saw a vision of God and cried out in wonder, "Surely the LORD is in this place; and I knew it not" (Genesis 28:16). Jacob had never been for one small division of a moment outside the circle of that all-pervading

Presence. But he knew it not. That was his trouble, and it is ours. Men do not know that God is here. What a difference it would make if they knew.

◇ ◇ ◇

We do not need to go "somewhere"
to find God, any more than the fish
needs to soar to find the ocean
or the eagle to plunge to find the air.
—*Rufus Jones*

◇ ◇ ◇

The Presence and the manifestation of the Presence are not the same. There can be the one without the other. God is here when we are wholly unaware of it. He is manifest only when and as we are aware of His presence. On our part, there must be surrender to the Spirit of God, for His work is to show us the Father and the Son. If we cooperate with Him in loving obedience, God will manifest Himself to us, and that manifestation will be the difference between a nominal Christian life and a life radiant with the light of His face.

Always, everywhere, God is present, and always He seeks to discover Himself to each one. He would reveal not only *that* He is, but *what* He is as well. He did not have to be persuaded to reveal Himself to Moses. "And the LORD descended in the cloud, and stood with him there, and proclaimed the name of the LORD" (Exodus 34:5). He not only made a verbal proclamation of His nature but He revealed His very Self to Moses so that the skin of Moses' face shone with the supernatural light. It will be a great moment for some of us when we begin to believe that God's promise of self-revelation is literally true, that He promised much, but no more than He intends to fulfill.

Never can father or mother embrace their child, nor any person embrace another with so much love as God Almighty embraces the rational soul.
—*Angela of Foligno*

◊   ◊   ◊

Our pursuit of God is successful just because He is forever seeking to manifest Himself to us. The revelation of God to any man is not God coming from a distance once upon a time to pay a brief and momentous visit to the man's

The presence of God is a fact of life. We may, by defying the purpose of God, insulate ourselves from that presence. We may, by unrepented sin, cut off the sense of God because we are clouded by a sense of guilt. We may, through no fault of our own, be unable to sense the God who is all about us. But the fact remains that He is with us all the time.

—*J.B. Phillips*

soul. Thus to think of it is to misunderstand it all. The approach of God to the soul or of the soul to God is not to be thought of in spatial terms at all. There is no idea of physical distance involved in the concept. It is not a matter of miles but of experience.

The soul loves and is loved in return; she seeks and is sought; she calls and is called. But in this, she lifts and is lifted up; she holds and is herself held; she clasps and she is closely embraced, and by the bond of love she unites herself to God, one with one, alone with Him.
—Saint Thomas Aquinas

To speak of being near to or far from God is to use language in a sense always understood when applied to our ordinary human relationships. A man may say, "I feel that my son is coming nearer to me as he gets older," and yet that son has lived by his father's side since he was born and has never been away from home more than a day or so in his entire life. What then can the father mean? Obviously he is speaking of *experience.* He means that the boy is coming to know him more intimately and with deeper understanding, that the barriers of thought and feeling between the two are disappearing, that father and son are becoming more closely united in mind and heart.

So when we sing, "Draw me nearer, nearer, nearer blessed Lord," we are not thinking of the nearness of place, but of the nearness of relationship. It is for increasing degrees of awareness that we pray, for a more perfect consciousness of the divine Presence. We need never shout across the spaces to an absent God. He is nearer than our own soul, closer than our most secret thoughts.

Nearer, still nearer, close to Thy heart,
Draw me, my Saviour, so precious Thou art;
Fold me, oh, fold me close to Thy breast,
Shelter me safe in that haven of rest,
Shelter me safe in that haven of rest.

Nearer, still nearer, Lord, to be Thine,
Sin, with its follies, I gladly resign,
All of its pleasures, pomp, and its pride.
Give me but Jesus, my Lord crucified,
Give me but Jesus, my Lord crucified.

Nearer, still nearer, while life shall last,
Till safe in glory my anchor is cast,
Through endless ages, ever to be
Nearer my Saviour, still nearer to Thee,
Nearer my Saviour, still nearer to Thee.
        —Lelia N. Morris

Day 16

Cultivating Spiritual Receptivity

Seek ye the LORD *while he may be found,*
call ye upon him while he is near.

Isaiah 55:6

For I know the thoughts that I think toward
you, saith the LORD, *thoughts of peace, and*
not of evil, to give you an expected end.
Then shall ye call upon me, and ye shall go
and pray unto me, and I will hearken unto
you.

Jeremiah 29:11-12

That they should seek the Lord, if haply
they might feel after him, and find him,
though he be not far from every one of us.

Acts 17:27

*W*hy do some persons "find" God in a way that
others do not? Why does
God manifest His presence to
some and let multitudes of others
struggle along in the half-light of
imperfect Christian experience?
Of course, the will of God is the

same for all. He has no favorites within His household. All He has ever done for any of His children He will do for all of His children. The difference lies not with God but with us.

Pick at random a score of great saints whose lives and testimonies are widely known. Let them be Bible characters or well-known Christians of post-biblical times. You will be struck instantly with the fact that the saints were not alike. Sometimes the unlikenesses were so great as to be positively glaring. How different, for example, was Moses from Isaiah; how different was Elijah from David; how unlike each other were John and Paul, St. Francis and Luther, Finney and Thomas à Kempis. The differences are as wide as human life itself—differences of race, nationality, education, temperament, habit and personal qualities. Yet they all walked, each in his day, upon a high road of spiritual living far above the common way.

Their differences must have been incidental and in the eyes of God of no significance. In some vital quality they must have been alike. What was it?

I venture to suggest that the one vital quality which they had in common was *spiritual receptivity*. Something in them was open to heaven, something which urged them Godward. Without attempting anything like a profound analysis, I shall say simply that they had spiritual awareness and that they went on to cultivate it until it became the biggest thing in their lives. They differed from the average person in that when they felt the inward longing they *did something about it*. They acquired the lifelong habit of spiritual response. They were not disobedient to the heavenly vision. As David put it neatly, "When thou saidst, Seek ye my face; my heart said unto thee, Thy face, LORD, will I seek" (Psalm 27:8).

As with everything good in human life, back of this receptivity is God. The sovereignty of God is here and is felt even by those who have not placed particular stress upon it theologically. The pious Michelangelo confessed this in a sonnet:

> *God does not communicate things to us so much as He just is Himself in us. We are the vessels, the containers, so that the first work after the new birth is to cultivate the habit of receptivity.*
>
> *—Norman Grubb*

> My unassisted heart is barren clay,
> That of its native self can nothing feed:
> Of good and pious works Thou are the seed,
> That quickens only where Thou sayest it
>   may:
> Unless Thou show to us Thine own true way
> No man can find it: Father! Thou must lead.

These words will repay study as the deep and serious testimony of a great Christian.

Important as it is that we recognize God working in us, I would yet warn against a too-great preoccupation with the thought. It is a sure road to sterile passivity. God will not hold us responsible to understand the mysteries of election, predestination and the divine sovereignty. The best and safest way to deal with these truths is to raise our eyes to God and in deepest reverence say, "O Lord, Thou knowest." Those things belong to the deep and mysterious Profound of God's omniscience. Prying into them may make theologians, but it will never make saints.

> *A saint is a creature of vast possibilities, knit into shape by the ruling personality of God.*
>
> *—Oswald Chambers*

Spirit of God, descend upon my heart;
Wean it from earth, through all its pulses move;
Stoop to my weakness, mighty as Thou art,
And make me love Thee as I ought to love.

I ask no dream, no prophet ecstasies,
No sudden rending of the veil of clay,
No angel visitant, no opening skies;
But take the dimness of my soul away.

Hast Thou not bid us love Thee, God and King?
All, all Thine own—soul, heart and strength
and mind.
I see Thy cross—there teach my heart to cling.
Oh, let me seek Thee, and oh, let me find.

Teach me to feel that Thou art always nigh;
Teach me the struggles of the soul to bear,
To check the rising doubt, the rebel sigh;
Teach me the patience of unanswered
prayer.

Teach me to love Thee as Thine angels love,
One holy passion filling all my frame;
The baptism of the heaven-descended Dove,
My heart an altar, and Thy love the flame.
—George Croly

101

~True Spirituality~

1. First is the desire to be holy rather than happy.

2. A man may be considered spiritual when he wants to see the honor of God advanced through his life.

3. The spiritual man wants to carry his cross.

4. Again a Christian is spiritual when he sees everything from God's viewpoint.

5. Another desire of the spiritual man is to die right rather than to live wrong.

6. The desire to see others advance at his expense is another mark of the spiritual man.

7. The spiritual man habitually makes eternity-judgments instead of time-judgments.

—AWT *in* That Incredible Christian

Day 17

Pursuing God

My flesh and my heart faileth: but God is the strength of my heart, and my portion for ever.

Psalm 73:26

As the hart panteth after the water brooks, so panteth my soul after thee, O God. My soul thirsteth for God, for the living God: when shall I come and appear before God?

Psalm 42:1-2

O God, thou art my God; early will I seek thee: my soul thirsteth for thee, my flesh longeth for thee in a dry and thirsty land, where no water is.

Psalm 63:1

Receptivity is not a single thing; rather, it is a compound, a blending of several elements within the soul. It is an affinity for, a bent toward, a sympathetic response to, a desire to have. From this it may be gathered that it can be present in degrees, that we may have little or more, depending upon the individual. It may be increased by exercise or destroyed by neglect. It is not a sovereign and irresistible force which comes upon us as a seizure from above. It is a gift of God, indeed, but one which must be recognized and cultivated as any other gift if we are to realize the purpose for which it was given.

Failure to see this is the cause of a very serious breakdown in modern evangelicalism. The idea of cultivation and exercise, so dear to the saints of old, has now no place in our total religious picture. It is too slow, too common. We now demand glamour and fast-flowing dramatic action. A generation of Christians reared among push buttons and automatic machines is impatient of slower and less direct methods of reaching their goals. We have been trying to apply machine-age methods to our relations with God. We read our chapter, have our short devotions and rush away,

Our nature hungers for God even when it broke with Him long ago, perhaps the more intensely the longer ago it was. It experiences a sort of famine. But the devil rides it and spurs it on, to distract it from its own need. He changes its hunger into haste. That is why people today are in such a hurry. Their speed is to distract their hunger.

—Louis Evely

hoping to make up for our deep inward bankruptcy by attending another gospel meeting or listening to another thrilling story told by a religious adventurer lately returned from afar.

The tragic results of this spirit are all about us: Shallow lives, hollow religious philosophies, the preponderance of the element of fun in gospel meetings, the glorification of men, trust in religious externalities, quasi-religious fellowships, salesmanship methods, the mistaking of dynamic personality for the power of the Spirit. These and such as these are the symptoms of an evil disease, a deep and serious malady of the soul.

> *Do you not know that your great sin is this: the all-pervading and eternal Presence is here, and you cannot feel Him?*
>
> *—AWT in* Who Put Jesus on the Cross?

For this great sickness that is upon us no one person is responsible, and no Christian is wholly free from blame. We have all contributed, directly or indirectly, to this sad state of affairs. We have been too blind to see, or too timid to speak out, or too self-satisfied to desire anything better than the poor, average diet with which others appear satisfied. To put it differently, we have accepted one another's notions, copied one another's lives and made one another's experiences the model for our own. And for a generation the trend has been downward. Now we have reached a low place of sand and burnt wire grass and, worst of all, we have made the Word of Truth conform to our experience and accepted this low plane as the very pasture of the blessed.

It will require a determined heart and more than a little courage to wrench ourselves loose from the grip of our times and return to biblical ways. But it can be done. Every now and then in the past Christians have had to do it. History has recorded several large-scale returns led by such men as St. Francis, Martin Luther and George Fox. Unfortunately, there seems to be no Luther or Fox on the horizon at present. Whether or not another such return may be expected before the coming of Christ is a question upon which Christians are not fully agreed, but that is not of too great importance to us now.

God designed the human machine to run on Himself. He Himself is the fuel our spirits were designed to burn, or the food our spirits were designed to feed on. There is no other.
—C.S. Lewis

What God in His sovereignty may yet do on a world-scale I do not claim to know. But what He will do for the plain man or woman who seeks His face I believe I do know and can tell others. Let any man turn to God in earnest, let him begin to exercise himself unto godliness, let him seek to develop his powers of spiritual receptivity by trust and obedience and humility, and the results will exceed anything he may have hoped in his leaner and weaker days.

Any man who by repentance and a sincere return to God will break himself out of the mold in which he has been held, and will go to the Bible itself for his spiritual standards, will be delighted with what he finds there.

Let us say it again: The universal Presence is a fact. God is here. The whole universe is alive with His life. And He is no strange or foreign God, but

No one questions the need of times of formal address to God, but few admit in any practical way the need of quiet waiting upon God, gazing into His face, feeling for His hand, listening for His voice. God has special confidences for each soul. Indeed, it would seem as though the deepest truths come only in moments of profound devotional silence and contemplation.

— Charles H. Brent

the familiar Father of our Lord Jesus Christ whose love has for these thousands of years enfolded the sinful race of men. And always He is trying to get our attention, to reveal Himself to us, to communicate with us. We have within us the ability to know Him if we will but respond to His overtures. (And this we call pursuing God!) We will know Him in increasing degree as our receptivity becomes more perfect by faith and love and practice.

O God and Father, I repent of my sinful preoccupation with visible things. The world has been too much with me. Thou hast been here and I knew it not. I have been blind to Thy presence. Open my eyes that I may behold Thee in and around me. For Christ's sake. Amen.

Day 18

God's Creative Voice

*In the beginning was the Word, and the
Word was with God, and the Word was God.
The same was in the beginning with God.
All things were made by him; and without
him was not any thing made that was made.
In him was life; and the life was the light of
men. And the light shineth in darkness; and
the darkness comprehended it not.*

John 1:1-5

*A*n intelligent, plain man, untaught in the truths
of Christianity, coming upon this text, would
likely conclude that John meant to teach that it is
the nature of God to speak, to communicate His
thoughts to others. And he would be right. A
word is a medium by which thoughts are ex-
pressed, and the application of the term to the
eternal Son leads us to believe
that self-expression is inherent in
the Godhead, that God is forever
seeking to speak Himself out to
His creation. The whole Bible
supports this idea. God is speak-

ing. Not God spoke, but *God is speaking*. He is, by His nature, continuously articulate. He fills the world with His speaking voice.

◇ ◇ ◇

The voice of the LORD is upon the waters: the
God of glory thundereth: the LORD is upon
many waters. The voice of the LORD is power-
ful; the voice of the LORD is full of majesty.
The voice of the LORD breaketh the cedars;
yea, the LORD breaketh the cedars of Lebanon.
He maketh them also to skip like a calf; Leba-
non and Sirion like a young unicorn. The
voice of the LORD divideth the flames of fire.
The voice of the LORD shaketh the wilderness;
the LORD shaketh the wilderness of Kadesh.
The voice of the LORD maketh the hinds to
calve, and discovereth the forests: and in his
temple doth every one speak of his glory.
Psalm 29:3-9

One of the great realities with which we have to deal is the voice of God in His world. The briefest and only satisfying cosmogony is this: "He spake, and it was done" (Psalm 33:9). The *why* of natural law is the loving voice of God immanent in His creation. And this word of God which brought all worlds into being cannot be understood to mean the Bible, for it is not a written or printed word at all, but the expression of the will of God is the breath of God filling the world with living potentiality. The voice of God is the most powerful force in nature, indeed the only force in nature, for all energy is here only because the power-filled Word is being spoken.

The Bible is the written Word of God, and because it is written it is confined and limited by the necessities of ink and paper and leather. The voice of God, however, is alive and free as the sovereign God is free. "The words that I speak unto you, they are spirit, and they are life" (John 6:63). The life is in the speaking words. God's word in the Bible can have power only because it corresponds to God's word in the universe. It is the present Voice which makes the written Word all-powerful. Otherwise it would lie locked in slumber within the covers of a book.

What man has written man may read;
But God fills every root and seed
With cryptic words too strangely set
For mortals to decipher yet.

— Charles Dalmon

We take a low and primitive view of things when we conceive of God at the creation coming into physical contact with things, shaping and fitting and building like a carpenter. The Bible teaches otherwise: "By the word of the LORD were the heavens made; and all the host of them by the breath of his mouth. . . . For he spake, and it was done; he commanded, and it stood fast" (Psalm 33:6, 9). "Through faith we understand that the worlds were framed by the word of God" (Hebrews 11:3). Again we must remember that God is referring here not to His written Word, but to His speaking Voice. His world-filling Voice is meant, that Voice which antedates the Bible by uncounted centuries, that Voice which has not been silent since the dawn of creation, but is sounding still throughout the full far reaches of the universe.

If the living voice of God were not speaking in the world and in the hearts of men, the written Word could have no real meaning for us. Because God is speaking in His world, we are able to hear Him speak in His Word.

—AWT in God Tells the Man Who Cares

The Word of God is quick and powerful. In the beginning He spoke to nothing, and it became *something*. Chaos heard it and became order; darkness heard it and became light. "And God said . . . and it was so" (Genesis 1:9). These twin phrases, as cause and effect, occur throughout the Genesis story of creation. The *said* accounts for the *so*. The *so* is the *said* put into the continuous present.

God is here and He is speaking—these truths

are back of all other Bible truths; without them there could be no revelation at all. God did not write a book and send it by messenger to be read at a distance by unaided minds. He spoke a Book and lives in His spoken words, constantly speaking His words and causing the power of them to persist across the years. God breathed on clay and it became a man; He breathes on men and they become clay. "Return, ye children of men" (Psalm 90:3) was the word spoken at the Fall by which God decreed the death of every man, and no added word has He needed to speak. The sad procession of mankind across the face of the earth from birth to the grave is proof that His original word was enough.

Lord, I have shut the door,
Speak now the word
Which in the din and throng
Could not be heard;
Hushed now my inner heart,
Whisper Thy will,
While I have come apart,
While all is still.

Lord, I have shut the door,
Here do I bow;
Speak, for my soul attent
Turns to Thee now.

Rebuke Thou what is vain,
Counsel my soul,
Thy holy will reveal,
My will control.
—William M. Runyan

Day 19

God's Inner Voice

There is hardly ever a complete silence in our soul. God is whispering to us well nigh incessantly. Whenever the sounds of the world die out in the soul, or sink low, then we hear these whisperings of God. He is always whispering to us, only we do not always hear because of the noise, hurry, and distraction which life causes as it rushes on.
—*Frederick W. Faber*

*W*e have not given sufficient attention to that deep utterance in the book of John, "That was the true Light, which lighteth every man that cometh into the world" (1:9). Shift the punctuation around as we will, the truth is still there: The Word of God affects the hearts of all men as light in the soul. In the hearts of all men the light shines, the Word sounds, and there is no escaping them. Something like this would of necessity be so if God is alive and in His world. And John says that it is so.

Even those persons who have never heard of the Bible have still been preached to with sufficient clarity to remove every excuse from their hearts forever. "Which shew the work of the law written in their hearts, their conscience also bearing witness, and their thoughts the mean while accusing or else excusing one another" (Romans 2:15). "For the invisible things of him from the creation of the world are clearly seen, being understood by the things that are made, even his eternal power and Godhead; so that they are without excuse" (1:20).

This universal Voice of God was by the ancient Hebrews often called Wisdom, and was said to be everywhere sounding and searching throughout the earth, seeking some response from the sons of men. The eighth chapter of Proverbs begins, "Doth not wisdom cry? and understanding put forth her voice?" The writer then pictures wisdom as a beautiful

When conscience begins to be awakened by God, we either become subtle hypocrites or saints, that is, either we let God's law working through conscience bring us to the place where we can be put right, or we begin to hoodwink ourselves, to affect a religious pose, not before other people, but before ourselves, in order to appease conscience—anything to be kept out of the real presence of God because wherever He comes, He disturbs.

— Oswald Chambers

woman standing "in the top of high places, by the way in the places of the paths" (8:2). She sounds her voice from every quarter so that no one may miss hearing it. "Unto you, O men, I call; and my voice is to the sons of man" (8:4). Then she pleads for the simple and the foolish to give ear to her words. It is spiritual responses for which this Wisdom of God is pleading, a response which she has always sought and is but rarely able to secure. The tragedy is that our eternal welfare depends upon our hearing and we have trained our ears not to hear.

This universal Voice has ever sounded, and it has often troubled men even when they did not understand the source of their fears. Could it be that this Voice distilling like a living mist upon the hearts of men has been the undiscovered cause of the troubled conscience and the longing for immortality confessed by millions since the dawn of recorded history? We need not fear to face up to this. The speaking Voice is a fact. How men have reacted to it is for any observer to note.

When God spoke out of heaven to our Lord, self-centered men who heard it explained it by natural causes, saying, "It thundered." This habit of explaining the Voice by appeals to natural law is at the very root of modern science. In the living, breathing cosmos there is a mysterious Something, too wonderful, too awful for any mind to understand. The believing man does not claim to understand. He falls to his knees and whispers, "God." The man of earth kneels also, but not to worship. He kneels to examine, to search, to find the cause and the how of things. Just now we happen to be living in a secular age. Our thought habits are those of the scientist, not those of the worshiper. We are more likely to explain than to adore. "It thundered," we exclaim, and go our earthly way. But still the Voice sounds and searches. The order and life of the world depend upon that Voice, but men are mostly too busy or too stubborn to give attention.

Every one of us has had experiences which we have not been able to explain—a sudden sense of loneliness, or a feeling of wonder or awe in the face of the universal vastness. Or we have had a fleeting visitation of light like an illumination from some other sun, giving us in a quick flash an as-

Does not all nature around me praise God? If I were silent, I should be an exception to the universe. Does not the thunder praise Him as it rolls like drums in the march of the God of armies? Do not the mountains praise Him when the woods upon their summits wave in adoration? Does not the lightning write His name in letters of fire? Has not the whole earth a voice? And shall I, can I, silent be?

— Charles H. Spurgeon

surance that we are from another world, that our origins are divine. What we saw there, or felt, or heard, may have been contrary to all that we had been taught in the schools and at wide variance with all our former beliefs and opinions. We were forced to suspend our acquired doubts while, for a moment, the clouds were rolled back and we saw and heard for ourselves. Explain such things as we will, I think we have not been fair to the facts until we allow at least the possibility that such experiences may arise from the presence of God in the world and His persistent effort to communicate with mankind. Let us not dismiss such an hypothesis too flippantly.

It is my own belief (and here I shall not feel bad if no one follows me) that every good and beautiful thing which man has produced in the world has been the result of his faulty and sin-blocked response to the creative Voice sounding over the earth. The moral philosophers who dreamed their high dreams of virtue, the religious thinkers who speculated about God and immortality, the poets and artists who created out of common stuff pure and lasting beauty: How can we explain them? It is not enough to say simply, "It was genius."

What then is genius? Could it be that a genius is a man haunted by the speaking Voice, laboring and striving like one possessed to achieve ends which he only vaguely understands? That the great man may have missed God in his labors, that he may even have spoken or written against God does not destroy the idea I am advancing. God's redemptive revelation in Scripture is necessary to saving faith and peace with God. Faith in a risen Savior is necessary if the vague stirrings toward immortality are to bring us to restful and satisfying communion with God. To me this is a plausible explanation of all that is best out of Christ. But you can be a good Christian and not accept my thesis.

The Voice of God is a friendly Voice. No one need fear to listen to it unless he has already made up his mind to resist it. The blood of Jesus has covered not only the human race but all creation as well. "And, having made peace through the blood of his cross, by him to reconcile all things unto himself; by him, I say, whether they be things in earth, or things in heaven" (Colossians 1:20). We may safely preach a friendly heaven. The heavens as well as the earth are filled with the good will of Him that dwelt in the bush. The perfect blood of atonement secures this forever.

> *The soul that has been enriched by communion with God will not be dismayed by isolation but will welcome solitude. He will seek not the crowd but the closet, and emerging will never walk alone, for he has unseen companionship.*
>
> *—Frances J. Roberts*

Whoever will listen will hear the speaking heaven. This is definitely not the hour when men take kindly to an exhortation to listen, for listening is not today a part of popular religion. We are at the opposite end of the pole from there. Religion has accepted the monstrous heresy that noise, size, activity and bluster make a man dear to God. But we may take heart. To a people caught in the tempest of the last great conflict God says, "Be still, and know that I am God" (Psalm 46:10), and still He says it, as if He means to tell us that our strength and safety lie not in noise but in silence.

Speak, Lord, in the stillness,
While I wait on Thee;
Hushed my heart to listen,
In expectancy.

Speak, O blessed Master,
In this quiet hour;
Let me see Thy face, Lord,
Feel Thy touch of power.

Speak, Thy servant heareth,
Be not silent, Lord;
Waits my soul upon Thee
For the quickening word.
                    —E. May Grimes

~The Power of Silence~

. . . how thoroughly it heals and how
fully pleasing it is to God. It is by silence
that the saints grew. It was because of
silence that the power of God dwelt in
them; because of silence that the mysteries of God were known to them.
— Father Ammonas

It is in lonely solitude that God delivers
His best thoughts, and the mind needs
to be still and quiet to receive them.
— Charles R. Swindoll

For thy great gift, O Father,
We thank Thee today—
The gift of silence;
For the rich, warm, generous silence
We thank Thee,
Wherein our souls,
Stunted and shrivelled and starved
In the arid desert of everyday hurry and
strain,
May rest, and quietly grow, and expand
Upward to Thee.
—John S. Hoyland

Day 20

God's Speaking Word

The Spirit breathes upon the Word,
And brings the truth to light,
Precepts and promises afford
A sanctifying light.

A glory gilds the sacred page,
Majestic like the sun,
It gives a light to every age;
It gives, but borrows none.

—William Cowper

Open thou mine eyes, that I may behold wondrous things out of thy law.

Psalm 119:18

It is important that we get still to wait on God. And it is best that we get alone, preferably with our Bible outspread before us. Then if we will we may draw near to God and begin to hear Him speak to us in our hearts. I think for the average person the progression will be something like this: First a sound as of a Presence walking in the garden. Then a voice, more intelligible, but still far from clear. Then the happy moment when the Spirit begins to illuminate the Scriptures, and that which had been only a sound, or at best a voice, now becomes an intelligible word, warm and intimate and clear as the word of a dear friend. Then will come life and light, and best of all, ability to see and rest in and embrace Jesus Christ as Savior and Lord and All.

> To be brought within the zone of God's voice is to be profoundly altered.
>
> — Oswald Chambers

The Bible will never be a living Book to us until we are convinced that God is articulate in His universe. To jump from a dead, impersonal world to a dogmatic Bible is too much for most people. They may admit that they *should* accept the Bible as the Word of God, and they may try to think of it as such, but they find it impossible to believe that the words there on the page are actually for them. A man may say, "These words are addressed to me," and yet in his heart not feel and know that they are. He is the victim of a divided psychology. He tries to think of God as mute everywhere else and vocal only in a book.

I believe that much of our religious unbelief is due to a wrong conception of and a wrong feeling for the Scriptures of Truth. A silent God suddenly began to speak in a book and when the book was finished lapsed back into silence again forever. Now we read the book as the record of what God said when He was for a brief time in a speaking mood. With notions like that in our heads how can we believe? The facts are that God is not silent, has never been silent. It is the nature of God to speak. The second Person of the Holy Trinity is called the *Word*. The Bible is the inevitable outcome of God's continuous speech. It is the infallible declaration of His mind for us put into our familiar human words.

I think a new world will arise out of the religious mists when we approach our Bible with the idea that it is not only a book which was once spoken, but a book which is *now speaking*. The prophets habitually said, "Thus *saith* the LORD." They meant their hearers to understand that God's speaking is in the continuous

Turn away mine eyes from beholding vanity; and quicken thou me in thy way.

Psalm 119:37

Great peace have they which love thy law: and nothing shall offend them.

Psalm 119:165

Thy word is a lamp unto my feet, and a light unto my path.

Psalm 119:105

Thy testimonies have I taken as an heritage for ever: for they are the rejoicing of my heart.

Psalm 119:111

present. We may use the past tense properly to indicate that at a certain time a certain word of God was spoken, but a word of God once spoken continues to be spoken, as a child once born continues to be alive or a world once created continues to exist. And those are but imperfect illustrations, for children die and worlds burn out, but the Word of our God endureth forever.

> *Nobody ever outgrows Scripture; the book widens and deepens with our years.*
>
> *— Charles H. Spurgeon*

If you would follow on to know the Lord, come at once to the open Bible expecting it to speak to you. Do not come with the notion that it is a *thing* which you may push around at your convenience. It is more than a thing; it is a voice, a word, the very Word of the living God.

Lord, teach me to listen. The times are noisy and my ears are weary with the thousand raucous sounds which continuously assault them. Give me the spirit of the boy Samuel when he said to Thee, "Speak, LORD, for thy servant heareth." Let me hear Thee speaking in my heart. Let me get used to the sound of Thy voice, that its tones may be familiar when the sounds of earth die away and the only sound will be the music of Thy speaking voice. Amen.

Day 21

The Central Place of Faith

Now faith is the substance of things hoped for, the evidence of things not seen.

Hebrews 11:1

So then faith cometh by hearing, and hearing by the word of God.

Romans 10:17

*L*et us think of our intelligent, plain man coming for the first time to the reading of the Scriptures. He approaches the Bible without any previous knowledge of what it contains. He is wholly without prejudice; he has nothing to prove and nothing to defend.

Such a man will not have read long until his mind begins to observe certain truths standing out from the page. They are the spiritual principles behind the record of God's dealings with men, and woven into the writings of holy men as they "were moved by the Holy Ghost" (2 Peter 1:21). As he reads on he might want to number these truths as they become clear to him and make a brief summary under each number. These summaries will be the tenets of his biblical creed. Further reading will not affect these points except to enlarge and strengthen them. Our man is finding out what the Bible actually teaches.

High up on the list of things which the Bible teaches will be the doctrine of *faith*. The place of weighty importance which the Bible gives to faith will be too plain for him to miss. He will very likely conclude that faith is all-important in the life of the soul. "Without faith it is impossible to please [God]" (Hebrews 11:6). Faith will get me anything, take me anywhere in the kingdom of God, but without faith there can be no approach to God, no forgiveness, no deliverance, no salvation, no communion, no spiritual life at all.

By the time our friend has reached the 11th chap-

I prayed for faith and thought that some day faith would come down and strike me like lightning. But faith did not seem to come. One day I read in the tenth chapter of Romans, "Faith cometh by hearing, and hearing by the word of God." I had up to this time closed my Bible and prayed for faith. I now opened my Bible and began to study, and faith has been growing ever since.

— Dwight L. Moody

ter of Hebrews the eloquent encomium which is there pronounced upon faith will not seem strange to him. He will have read Paul's powerful defense of faith in his Roman and Galatian epistles. Later, if he goes on to study church history, he will understand the amazing power in the teachings of the Reformers as they showed the central place of faith in the Christian religion.

Now if faith is so vitally important, if it is an indispensable *must* in our pursuit of God, it is perfectly natural that we should be deeply concerned over whether or not we possess this most precious gift. And our minds being what they are, it is inevitable that sooner or later we should get around to inquiring after the nature of faith. "What *is* faith?" would lie close to the question, "Do I *have* faith?" and would demand an answer if it were anywhere to be found.

Faith wears every-day clothes and proves herself in life's ordinary situations.

— Bertha Munro

Almost all who preach or write on the subject of faith have much the same things to say concerning it. They tell us that it is believing a promise, that it is taking God at His word, that it is reckoning the Bible to be true and stepping out upon it. The rest of the book or sermon is usually taken up with stories of persons who have had their prayers answered as a result of their faith. These answers are mostly direct gifts of a practical and temporal nature such as health, money, physical protection or success in business. Or if the teacher is of a philosophic turn of mind he may take another course and lose us in a welter of metaphysics or snow us under with psychological jargon as he defines and redefines, paring the slender hair of faith thinner and thinner till it disappears in gossamer shavings at last. When he is finished we get up disappointed and go out "by that same door where in we went." Surely there must be something better than this.

> I am so made that worry and anxiety are sand in the machinery of life: faith is oil.
> — E. Stanley Jones

In Scripture there is practically no effort made to define faith. Outside of a brief 14-word definition in Hebrews 11:1, I know of no biblical definition. Even there faith is defined functionally, not philosophically; that is, it is a statement of what faith is *in operation, not* what it is *in essence.* It assumes the presence of faith and shows what it results in, rather than what it is. We will be wise to go just that far and attempt to go no further. We are told from whence it comes and by what means: "Faith . . . is the gift of God" (Ephesians 2:8) and "Faith cometh by hearing, and hearing by the word of God" (Romans 10:17). This much is clear, and, to paraphrase Thomas à Kempis, "I had rather exercise faith than know the definition thereof."

~Tozer—Thoughts on Faith~

We must have faith; and let us not apologize for it, for faith is an organ of knowledge and can tell us more about ultimate reality than all the findings of science. We are not opposed to science, but we recognize its proper limitations and refuse to stop where it is compelled to stop. The Bible tells of another world too fine for the instruments of scientific research to discover. By faith we engage that world and make it ours. It is accessible to us through the blood of the everlasting covenant. If we will believe we may even now enjoy the presence of God and the ministry of His heavenly messengers. Only unbelief can rob us of this royal privilege.

— Of God and Men

Faith never asks questions when it has been established that God has spoken.
—The Root of the Righteous

True faith is never found alone; it is always accompanied by expectation. The man who believes the promises of God expects to see them fulfilled. Where there is no expectation there is no faith.
— God Tells the Man Who Cares

It takes real faith to begin to live the life of heaven while still upon the earth, for this requires that we rise above the law of moral gravitation and bring to our every-day living the high wisdom of God. And since this wisdom is contrary to that of the world, conflict is bound to result. This, however, is a small price to pay for the inestimable privilege of following Christ.
— Born After Midnight

Real faith is not the stuff dreams are made of; rather it is tough, practical and altogether realistic.
— God Tells the Man Who Cares

Faith reposes on the character of God and if we believe that God is perfect we must conclude that His ways are perfect also.
— Born After Midnight

Day 22

Operational Faith

Faith is a grasping of Almighty power;
The hand of man laid on the arm of God;
The grand and blessed hour
In which the things, impossible to me,
Become the possible, O Lord, through Thee.
—*Anna E. Hamilton*

*W*hen the words "faith is" or their equivalent occur I ask that they be understood to refer to what faith is in operation as exercised by a believing man. Right here we drop the notion of definition and think about faith as it may be experienced in action. The complexion of our thoughts will be practical, not theoretical.

In a dramatic story in the book of Numbers (21:4–9) faith is seen in action. Israel became discouraged and spoke against God, and the Lord sent fiery serpents among them. "And they bit the people; and much people of Israel died" (21:6). Then Moses sought the Lord for them and He heard and gave them a remedy against the bite of the serpents. He commanded Moses to make a serpent of brass and put it upon a pole in sight of all the people, "and it shall come to pass, that every one that is bitten, when he looketh upon it, shall live" (21:8). Moses obeyed, "and it came to pass, that if a serpent had bitten any man, when he beheld the serpent of brass, he lived" (21:9).

> No image but the image of God can fit our soul; every other seal is too narrow, too shallow for it.
>
> —John Donne

In the New Testament this important bit of history is interpreted for us by no less an authority than our Lord Jesus Christ Himself. He is explaining to His hearers how they may be saved. He tells them that it is by believing. Then to make it clear He refers to this incident in the book of Numbers. "As Moses lifted up the serpent in the wilderness, even so must the Son of man be lifted up: That whosoever believeth in him should not perish, but have eternal life" (John 3:14–15).

Our plain man, in reading this, would make an important discovery. He would notice that *look* and *believe* are synonymous terms. "Looking" on the Old Testament serpent is identical with "believing" on the New Testament Christ. That is, the *looking* and the *believing* are the same thing. And he would understand that, while Israel looked with their external eyes, believing is done with the heart. I think he would conclude that *faith is the gaze of a soul upon a saving God.*

When he had seen this he would remember passages he had read before, and their meaning would come flooding over him. "They looked unto him, and were lightened: and their faces were not ashamed" (Psalm 34:5). "Unto thee lift I up mine eyes, O thou that dwellest in the heavens. Behold, as the eyes of servants look unto the hand of their masters, and as the eyes of a maiden unto the hand of her mistress; so our eyes wait upon the LORD our God, until that he have mercy upon us" (123:1-2). Here the man seeking mercy looks straight at the God of mercy and never takes his eyes away from Him till He grants mercy. And our Lord Himself looked always at God. "Looking up to heaven, he blessed, and brake, and gave the loaves to his disciples" (Matthew 14:19). Indeed, Jesus taught that He wrought His works by always keeping His inward eyes upon His Father. His power lay in His continuous look at God (John 5:19–21).

It is right that you should begin again every day. There is no better way to finish the spiritual life than to be ever beginning.
—St. Francis of Sales

135

In full accord with the few texts we have quoted is the whole tenor of the inspired Word. It is summed up for us in the Hebrew epistle when we are instructed to run life's race "looking unto Jesus the author and finisher of our faith" (Hebrews 12:2). From all this we learn that faith is not a once-done act, but a continuous gaze of the heart at the Triune God.

To adore God in truth is to admit that our nature is just the opposite of His. Yet, He is willing to make us like Him, if we desire it. Who would be so rash as to neglect, even for a moment, the respect, the love, the service, and the continual adoration that we owe Him?

—Brother Lawrence

Believing, then, is directing the heart's attention to Jesus. It is lifting the mind to "behold the Lamb of God" (John 1:29), and never ceasing that beholding for the rest of our lives. At first this may be difficult, but it becomes easier as we look steadily at His wondrous person, quietly and without strain. Distractions may hinder, but once the heart is committed to Him, after each brief excursion away from Him, the attention will return again and rest upon Him like a wandering bird coming back to its window.

I would emphasize this one committal, this one great volitional act which establishes the heart's intention to gaze forever upon Jesus. God takes this intention for our choice and makes what allowances He must for the thousand distractions which beset us in this evil world. He knows that we have set the direction of our hearts toward Jesus, and we can know it too, and comfort ourselves with the knowledge that a habit of soul is forming which will become, after a while, a sort of spiritual reflex requiring no more conscious effort on our part.

Faith is the least self-regarding of the virtues. It is by its very nature scarcely conscious of its own existence. Like the eye which sees everything in front of it and never sees itself, faith is occupied with the Object upon which it rests and pays no attention to itself at all. While we are looking at God we do not see ourselves—blessed riddance. The man who has struggled to purify himself and has had nothing but repeated failures will experience real relief when he stops tinkering with his soul and looks away to the perfect One. While he

Beware of believing that the human soul is simple, or that human life is simple. Our relationship to God in Christ is the only simple thing there is. If the devil succeeds in making this relationship complicated, then the human soul and human life will appear to be simple; whereas in reality they are far too complex for us to touch.

— Oswald Chambers

looks at Christ, the very things he has so long been trying to do will be getting done within him. It will be God working in him to will and to do.

Faith is not in itself a meritorious act; the merit is in the One toward Whom it is directed. Faith is a redirecting of our sight, a getting out of the focus of our own vision and getting God into focus. Sin has twisted our vision inward and made it self-regarding. Unbelief has put self where God should be, and is perilously close to the sin of Lucifer who said, "I will set my throne above the throne of God." Faith looks *out* instead of *in* and the whole life falls into line.

All this may seem too simple. But we have no apology to make. To those who would seek to climb into heaven after help or descend into hell, God says, "The word is nigh thee, even . . . the word of faith" (Romans 10:8). The Word induces us to lift up our eyes unto the Lord and the blessed work of faith begins.

> *O Lord, I have heard a good word inviting me to look away to Thee and be satisfied. My heart longs to respond, but sin has clouded my vision till I see Thee but dimly. Be pleased to cleanse me in Thine own precious blood, and make me inwardly pure, so that I may with unveiled eyes gaze upon Thee all the days of my earthly pilgrimage. Then shall*

I be prepared to behold Thee in full splendor in the day when Thou shalt appear to be glorified in Thy saints and admired in all them that believe. Amen.

Day 23

The Gaze of the Soul

My goal is God Himself, not joy, nor peace,
Nor even blessing, but Himself, my God.
'Tis His to lead me there, not mine, but His—
"At any cost, dear Lord, by any road!"
                                          —F. Brook

My soul longeth, yea, even fainteth for the
courts of the LORD: my heart and my flesh
crieth out for the living God.
                                          Psalm 84:2

*W*hen we lift our inward eyes to gaze upon God we are sure to meet friendly eyes gazing back at us, for it is written that the eyes of the Lord run to and fro throughout all the earth. The sweet language of experience is "Thou God seest me" (Genesis 16:13). When the eyes of the soul looking out meet the eyes of God looking in, heaven has begun right here on this earth.

Nicholas of Cusa wrote 400 years ago:

When all my endeavor is turned toward Thee because

all Thy endeavor is turned toward me; when I look unto Thee alone with all my attention, nor ever turn aside the eyes of my mind, because Thou dost enfold me with Thy constant regard; when I direct my love toward Thee alone because Thou, who art Love's self hast turned Thee toward me alone. And what, Lord, is my life, save that embrace wherein Thy delightsome sweetness doth so lovingly enfold me?[1]

> *To fall in love with God is the greatest of all romances! To seek Him is the greatest of all achievements! To find Him is the greatest human achievement!*
> —*Raphael Simon*

I should like to say more about this old man of God. He is not much known today anywhere among Christian believers, and among current fundamentalists he is known not at all. I feel that we could gain much from a little acquaintance with men of his spiritual flavor and the school of Christian thought which they represent. Christian literature, to be accepted and approved by evangelical leaders of our times, must follow very closely the same train of thought, a kind of

---

[1] Nicholas of Cusa, *The Vision of God*, E.P. Dutton & Co., Inc., New York, 1928. This and the following quotations used by permission of the publishers.

"party line" from which it is scarcely safe to depart. A half-century of this in America has made us smug and content. We imitate each other with slavish devotion. Our most strenuous efforts are put forth to try to say the same thing that everyone around us is saying—and yet to find an excuse for saying it, some little safe variation on the approved theme or, if no more, at least a new illustration.

Nicholas was a true follower of Christ, a lover of the Lord, radiant and shining in his devotion to the person of Jesus. His theology was orthodox but fragrant and sweet as everything about Jesus might properly be expected to be. His conception of eternal life, for instance, is beautiful in itself

Think often on God, by day, by night, in your business, and even in your diversions. He is always near you and with you; leave Him not alone. You would think it rude to leave a friend alone who came to visit you; why, then, must God be neglected?

—Brother Lawrence

and, if I mistake not, is nearer in spirit to John 17:3 than that which is current among us today. Life eternal, says Nicholas, is

nought other than that blessed regard
wherewith Thou never ceasest to behold

143

me, yes, even the secret places of my soul. With Thee, to behold is to give life; 'tis unceasingly to impart sweetest love of Thee; 'tis to inflame me to love of Thee by love's imparting, and to feed me by inflaming, and by feeding to kindle my yearning, and by kindling to make me drink of the dew of gladness, and by drinking to infuse in me a fountain of life, and by infusing to make it increase and endure.[2]

Now, if faith is the gaze of the heart at God, and if this gaze is but the raising of the inward eyes to meet the all-seeing eyes of God, then it follows that it is one of the easiest things possible to do. It would be like God to make the most vital thing easy and place it within the range of possibility for the weakest and poorest of us.

Several conclusions may fairly be drawn from all this. The simplicity of it, for instance. Since believing is looking, it can be done without special equipment or religious paraphernalia. God has seen to it that the one life-and-death essential can never be subject to the caprice of accident. Equipment can break down or get lost, water can leak away, records can be destroyed by fire, the minister can be delayed or the church can burn down.

---

[2] *The Vision of God.*

All these are external to the soul and are subject to accident or mechanical failure. But *looking* is of the heart and can be done successfully by any man standing up or kneeling down or lying in his last agony a thousand miles from any church.

Since believing is looking it can be done *any time*. No season is superior to another season for this sweetest of all acts. God never made salvation depend upon new moons or holy days or sabbaths. A man is not nearer to Christ on Easter Sunday than he is, say, on Saturday, August 3, or Monday, October 4. As long as Christ sits on the mediatorial throne, every day is a good day and all days are days of salvation.

Neither does *place* matter to this blessed work of believing God. Lift your heart and let it rest upon Jesus and you are instantly in a sanctuary though it be a Pullman berth or a factory or a kitchen. You can see God from anywhere if your mind is set to love and obey Him.

Now, someone may ask, "Is not this of which you speak for special persons such as monks or

> *The time of business does not differ from the time of prayer; and in the noise and clatter of my kitchen, while several persons are at the same time calling for different things, I possess God in as great tranquility as if I were upon my knees.*
>
> *—Brother Lawrence*

ministers who have, by the nature of their calling, more time to devote to quiet meditation? I am a busy worker and have little time to spend alone." I am happy to say that the life I describe is for every one of God's children regardless of calling. It is, in fact, happily practiced every day by many hard-working persons and is beyond the reach of none.

We must not think of ourselves as ordinary people. We are not natural men; we are born again. God has given us His Holy Spirit.

—D. Martyn Lloyd-Jones

So faith bounds forward to its goal in God,
And love can trust her Lord to lead her there;
Upheld by Him, my soul is following hard,
Till God hath full fulfilled my deepest prayer.

No matter if the way be sometimes dark,
No matter though the cost be oft-times great,
He knoweth how I best shall reach the mark—
The way that leads to Him must needs be strait.

One thing I know, I cannot say Him nay;
One thing I do, I press towards my Lord;
My God my glory here from day to day,
And in the glory there my Great Reward.
                                    —F. Brook

Day 24

A New Level of Spirituality

Tune me, O Lord, into one harmony
With Thee, one full responsive vibrant chord;
Unto Thy praise, all love and melody,
Tune me, O Lord.
— Christina Georgina Rossetti

*M*any have found the secret of which I speak and, without giving much thought to what is going on within them, constantly practice this habit of inwardly gazing upon God. They know that something inside their hearts sees God. Even when they are compelled to withdraw their conscious attention in order to engage in earthly affairs, there is within them a secret communion always going on. Let their attention but be released for a moment from necessary business and it flies at once to God again. This has been the testimony of many Christians, so many that even as I state it thus I have a feeling that I am quoting, though from whom or from how many I cannot possibly know.

I do not want to leave the impression that the ordinary means of grace have no value. They most assuredly have. Private prayer should be practiced by every Christian. Long periods of Bible meditation will purify our gaze and direct it; church attendance will enlarge our outlook and increase our love for others. Service and work and activity—all are good and should be engaged in by every Christian. But at the bottom of all these things, giving meaning to them, will be the inward habit of beholding God. A new set of eyes (so to speak) will develop within us enabling us to be looking at God while our outward eyes are seeing the scenes of this passing world.

> *My way is very simple. My soul lives on God, by a glance of love between Him and myself. By this glance God gives Himself to me, and I give myself to Him. This is my habitual state, that in which God has placed me.*
>
> —*Lucie Christine*

Someone may fear that we are magnifying private religion out of all proportion, that the "us" of the New Testament is being displaced by a selfish "I." Has it ever occurred to you that 100 pianos all tuned to the same fork are automatically tuned to each other? They are of one accord by being tuned, not to each other, but to another standard to which one must individually bow. So 100 worshipers meeting together, each one looking away to Christ, are in heart nearer to each other than they could possibly be were they to become "unity" conscious and turn their eyes away from God to strive for closer fellowship. Social religion is perfected when private religion is purified. The body becomes stronger as its members become healthier. The whole church of God gains when the members that compose it begin to seek a better and a higher life.

All the foregoing presupposes true repentance and a full committal of the life to God. It is hardly necessary to mention this, for only persons who have made such a committal will have read this far.

When the habit of inwardly gazing Godward becomes fixed within us, we shall be ushered onto a new level of spiritual life more in keeping with the promises of God and the mood of the New Testament. The Triune God will be our dwelling place even while our feet walk the low road of simple duty here among men. We will have found life's *summum bonum* indeed.

Dispose our soul for tranquility, O God, that the loving knowledge of contemplation may the more grow and the soul will feel it and relish it more than all other things whatever; because it brings with it peace and rest, sweetness and delight, without trouble.

—St. John of the Cross

There is the source of all delights that can be desired; not only can nought better be thought out by men and angels, but nought better can exist in any mode of being! For it is the absolute maximum of every rational desire, than which a greater cannot be.[1]

God fully expects the church of Jesus Christ to prove itself a miraculous group in the very midst of a hostile world. Christians of necessity must be in contact with the world but in being and spirit ought to be separated from the world—and as such, we should be the most amazing people in the world.
—AWT in I Call It Heresy!

O my God, let me walk in the way of love which knoweth not how to seek self in anything whatsoever. O sight to be wished, desired and longed for, because once to have seen Thee is to have learned all things! Nothing can bring us to this sight but love. O Lord, give this love into my soul, that I may never more live nor breathe, but out of a pure love of Thee, my all and only good. Amen.
—Dame Gertrude More

---

[1] *The Vision of God.*

~Thoughts from Tozer on . . .~

Private prayer:

Retire from the world each day to some private spot, even if it be only the bedroom (for a while I retreated to the furnace room for want of a better place). Stay in the secret place till the surrounding noises begin to fade out of your heart and a sense of God's presence envelops you. Deliberately tune out the unpleasant sounds and come out of your closet determined not to hear them. Listen for the inward Voice till you learn to recognize it. Stop trying to compete with others. Give yourself to God and then be what and who you are without regard to what others think. Reduce your interests to a few. Don't try to know what will be of no service to you. Avoid the digest type of mind—short bits of unrelated facts, cute stories and bright sayings. Learn to pray inwardly every moment. After a while you can do this even while you work. Practice candor, childlike honesty, humility. Pray for a single eye. Read less, but read more of what is important to your inner life. Never let your mind remain scattered for very long. Call home your roving thoughts. Gaze on Christ with the eyes of your soul. Practice spiritual concentration.

— Of God and Men

Bible reading:

The Spirit-filled walk demands that we live in the Word of God as a fish lives in the sea. By this I do not mean that we study the Bible merely, nor that we take a "course" in Bible doctrine. I mean that we should "meditate day and night" in the sacred Word, that we should love it and feast upon it and digest it every hour of the day and night.

—The Divine Conquest

We find the Bible difficult because we try to read it as we would read any other book, and it is not the same as any other book.

— Man: The Dwelling Place of God

Here's how the file card works when it gets into the Christian life and begins to create mental habits: It divides the Bible into sections fitted to the days of the year and compels the Christian to read according to rule. No matter what the Holy Spirit may be trying to say to a man, still he goes on reading where the card tells him, dutifully checking it off each day.

Every Spirit-led saint knows that there are times when he is held by an inward pressure to one chapter, or even one verse, for days at a time while he wrestles with God till some truth does its work within him. To leave that present passage to follow a pre-arranged reading schedule is for him wholly impossible. He is in the land of the free Spirit, and reality is appearing before him to break and humble and lift and liberate and cheer. But only the free soul can know the glory of this. To this the heart bound by system will be forever a stranger.

— Of God and Men

Service:

Fellowship with God leads straight to obedience and good works. That is the divine order and it can never be reversed.

— Born after Midnight

No one can long worship God in spirit and in truth before the obligation to holy service becomes too strong to resist.

— Born after Midnight

In Christian service motive is everything, for it is motive that gives to every moral act its final quality.
—The Next Chapter
After the Last

Church attendance:

In the average church service the most real thing is the shadowy unreality of everything. The worshiper sits in a state of suspended mentation; a kind of dreamy numbness creeps upon him; he hears words but they do not register, he cannot relate them to anything on his own life-level. He is conscious of having entered a kind of half-world; his mind surrenders itself to a more or less pleasant mood which passes with the benediction leaving no trace behind. It does not affect anything in his everyday life. He is aware of no power, no Presence, no spiritual reality. There is simply nothing in his experience corresponding to the things which he heard from the pulpit or sang in the hymns.
— Divine Conquest

A man may attend church for a lifetime and be none the better for it.
— Born After Midnight

According to the Scriptures the Church is the habitation of God through the Spirit, and as such is the most important organism beneath the sun. She is not one more good institution along with the home, the state and the school; she is the most vital of all institutions— the only one that can claim a heavenly origin.
— God Tells the Man
Who Cares

The Church must examine herself constantly to see if she be in the faith; she must engage in severe self-criticism with a cheerful readiness to make amends; she must live in a state of perpetual penitence, seeking God with her whole heart; she must constantly check her life and conduct against the Holy Scriptures and bring her life into line with the will of God.

— Of God and Men

We are in real need of a reformation that will lead to revival among the churches, but the Church is not dead, neither is it dying. The Church cannot die.

— Man: The Dwelling Place of God

Day 25

The Exaltation of God

Be thou exalted, O God, above the heavens;
let thy glory be above all the earth.

Psalm 57:5

Be thou exalted, LORD, in thine own
strength: so will we sing and praise thy
power.

Psalm 21:13

I will meditate also of all thy work, and talk
of thy doings. Thy way, O God, is in the
sanctuary: who is so great a God as our
God?

Psalm 77:12-13

Thou art my God, and I will praise thee:
thou art my God, I will exalt thee.

Psalm 118:28

*J*t is true that order in nature
depends upon right relationships; to achieve harmony each
thing must be in its proper position relative to each other thing.
In human life it is not otherwise.

I have hinted before that the cause of all our human miseries is a radical moral dislocation, an upset in our relation to God and to each other. For whatever else the Fall may have been, it was certainly a sharp change in man's relation to his Creator. He adopted toward God an altered attitude, and by so doing destroyed the proper Creator-creature relation in which, unknown to him, his true happiness lay. Essentially, salvation is the restoration of a right relation between man and his Creator, a bringing back to normal of the Creator-creature relation.

> Worship is the highest and noblest act that any person can do. When men worship, God is satisfied! And when you worship, you are fulfilled!
>
> — Raymond C. Ortlund

A satisfactory spiritual life will begin with a complete change in relation between God and the sinner; not a judicial change merely, but a conscious and experienced change affecting the sinner's whole nature. The atonement in Jesus' blood makes such a change judicially possible and the working of the Holy Spirit makes it emotionally satisfying. The story of the prodigal son perfectly illustrates this latter phase. He had brought a world of trouble upon himself by forsaking the position which he had properly held as son of his father. At bottom of his restoration was nothing more than a reestablishing of the father-son relation which had existed from his birth and had been altered temporarily by his act of sinful rebellion. This story overlooks the legal aspects of redemption, but it makes beautifully clear the experiential aspects of salvation.

In determining relationships we must begin somewhere. There must be somewhere a fixed center against which everything else is measured, where the law of relativity does not enter and we can say "IS" and make no allowances. Such a center is God. When God would make His name known to mankind He could find no better word than "I AM." When He speaks in the first person He says, "I AM"; when we speak *of* Him we say, "He is"; when we speak *to* Him we say, "Thou art." Everyone and everything else measures from that fixed point. "I AM THAT I AM," says God, "I change not."

As the sailor locates his position on the sea by "shooting" the sun, so we may get our moral bearings by looking at God. We must begin with God.

The fellowship of God is delightful beyond all telling. He communes with His redeemed ones in an easy, uninhibited fellowship that is restful and healing to the soul. He is not sensitive nor selfish nor temperamental. What He is today we shall find Him tomorrow and the next day and the next year.

—AWT *in* **The Root of the Righteous**

We are right when, and only when, we stand in a right position relative to God, and we are wrong so far and so long as we stand in any other position.

Much of our difficulty as seeking Christians stems from our unwillingness to take God as He is and adjust our lives accordingly. We insist upon trying to modify Him and to bring Him nearer to our own image. The flesh whimpers against the rigor of God's inexorable sentence and begs like Agag for a little mercy, a little indulgence of its carnal ways. It is no use. We can get a right start only by accepting God as He is and learning to love Him for what He is. As we go on to know Him better we shall find it a source of unspeakable joy that God is just what He is. Some of the most rapturous moments we know will be those we spend in reverent admiration of the Godhead. In those holy moments the very thought of change in Him will be too painful to endure.

> The one essential condition of human existence is that man should always be able to bow down before something infinitely great. The Infinite and the Eternal are as essential for man as the little planet on which he dwells.
>
> — *Fyodor Dostoyevski*

So let us begin with God. Back of all, above all, before all is God; first in sequential order, above in rank and station, exalted in dignity and honor. As the self-existent One He gave being to all things, and all things exist out of Him and for Him. "Thou art worthy, O Lord, to receive glory and honour and power: for thou hast created all things, and for thy pleasure they are and were created" (Revelation 4:11).

Every soul belongs to God and exists by His pleasure. God being who and what He is, and we being who and what we are, the only thinkable relation between us is one of full Lordship on His part and complete submission on ours. We owe Him every honor that is in our power to give Him. Our everlasting grief lies in giving Him anything less.

The pursuit of God will embrace the labor of bringing our total personality into conformity to His. And this not judicially, but actually. I do not here refer to the act of justification by faith in Christ. I speak of a voluntary exalting of God to His proper station over us and a willing surrender of our whole being to the place of worshipful submission which the Creator-creature circumstance makes proper.

Silent worship is healing; it is uniting; it cleanses, challenges, stimulates. It helps us to get down to those deeper currents of the soul that are so often neglected in life's hurry and bustle; it enables us to center down into fellowship with the Eternal and to hear the still small voice of God.

— Gerald K. Hibbert

The moment we make up our minds that we are going on with this determination to exalt God over all, we step out of the world's parade. We shall find ourselves out of adjustment to the ways of the world, and increasingly so as we make progress in the holy way. We shall acquire a new viewpoint; a new and different psychology will be formed within us; a new power will begin to surprise us by its upsurgings and its outgoings.

Our break with the world will be the direct outcome of our changed relation to God. For the world of fallen men does not honor God. Millions call themselves by His name, it is true, and pay some token respect to Him, but a simple test will show how little He is really honored among them. Let the average man be put to the proof on the question of who or what is *above*, and his true position will be exposed. Let him be forced into making a choice between God and money, between God and men, between God and personal ambition, God and self, God and human love, and God will take second place every time. Those other things will be exalted above. However the man may protest, the proof is in the choices he makes day after day throughout his life.

"Be thou exalted" (Psalm 21:13) is the language of victorious spiritual experience. It is a little key to unlock the door to great treasures of grace. It is central in the life of God in the soul. Let the seeking man reach a place where life and lips join to say continually "Be thou exalted," and a thousand minor problems will be solved at once. His Christian life ceases to be the complicated thing it had been before and becomes the very essence of simplicity. By the exercise of his will he has set his course, and on that course he will stay as if guided by an automatic pilot. If blown off course for a moment by some adverse wind, he will surely return again as by a secret bent of the soul. The hidden motions of the Spirit are working in his favor, and "the stars in their courses" (Judges 5:20) fight for him. He has met his life problem at its center, and everything else must follow along.

O God, be Thou exalted over my possessions. Nothing of earth's treasures shall seem dear unto me if only Thou art glorified in my life. Be Thou exalted over my friendships. I am determined that Thou shalt be above all, though I must stand deserted and alone in the midst of the earth. Be Thou exalted above my comforts. Though it mean the loss of bodily comforts and the carrying of heavy crosses, I shall keep my vow made this day before Thee. Be Thou exalted over my reputation. Make me ambitious to please Thee even if as a result I must sink into obscurity and my name be forgotten as a dream.

Day 26

God's Claim to Preeminence

> Thine am I, I was born for Thee,
> What wouldst Thou, Master, make of me?
> Give me death or give me life
> Give health or give infirmity
> Give honor or give obloquy
> Give peace profound or daily strife,
> Weakness or strength add to my life;
> Yes, Lord, my answer still shall be
> What wilt Thou, Master, have of me?
> —*Teresa of Avila*

*L*et no one imagine that he will lose anything of human dignity by this voluntary sellout of his all to his God. He does not by this degrade himself as a man; rather he finds his right place of high honor as one made in the image of his Creator. His deep disgrace lay in his moral derangement, his unnatural usurpation of the place of God. His honor will be proved by restoring again that stolen throne. In exalting God over all he finds his own highest honor upheld.

Anyone who might feel reluctant to surrender his will to the will of another should remember Jesus' words, "Whosoever committeth sin is the servant of sin" (John 8:34). We must of necessity be servant to someone, either to God or to sin. The sinner prides himself on his independence, completely overlooking the fact that he is the weak slave of the sins that rule his members. The man who surrenders to Christ exchanges a cruel slave driver for a kind and gentle Master whose yoke is easy and whose burden is light.

Made as we were in the image of God, we scarcely find it strange to take again our God as our All. God was our original habitat and

The well-defined spiritual life is not only the highest life, but it is also the most easily lived. The whole cross is more easily carried than the half. It is the man who tries to make the best of both worlds who makes nothing of either. And he who seeks to serve two masters misses the benediction of both. Both he who has taken his stand, who has drawn a boundary-line sharp and deep about his religious life, who has marked off all beyond as forever forbidden ground to him, finds the yoke easy and the burden light. For this forbidden environment comes to be as if it were not. . . . And the balm of death numbing his lower nature releases him for the scarce disturbed communion of a higher life. So even here to die is gain.

—Henry Drummond

our hearts cannot but feel at home when they enter again that ancient and beautiful abode.

I hope it is clear that there is a logic behind God's claim to preeminence. That place is His by every right in earth or heaven. While we take to ourselves the place that is His, the whole course of our lives is out of joint. Nothing will or can restore order till our hearts make the great decision: God shall be exalted above.

"Them that honour me I will honour" (1 Samuel 2:30), said God once to a priest of Israel, and that ancient law of the kingdom stands today unchanged by the passing of time or the changes of dispensation. The whole Bible and every page of history proclaim the perpetuation of that law. "If any man serve me, him will my Father honour," (John 12:26), said our Lord Jesus, tying in the old with the new and revealing the essential unity of His ways with men.

Sometimes the best way to see a thing is to look at its opposite. Eli and his sons are placed in the priesthood with the stipulation that they honor God in their lives and ministrations. This they fail to do, and God sends Samuel to announce the consequences. Unknown to Eli this law of reciprocal honor has been all the while secretly working, and now the time has come for judgment to fall. Hophni and Phineas, the degenerate priests, fall in battle; the wife of Hophni dies in childbirth; Israel flees before her enemies; the ark of God is captured by the Philistines and the old man Eli falls backward and dies of a broken neck. Thus stark, utter tragedy followed upon Eli's failure to honor God.

Now over against this set almost any Bible character who honestly tried to glorify God in his earthly walk. See how God winked at weakness and overlooked failures as He poured upon His servants grace and blessing untold. Let it be Abraham, Jacob, David, Daniel, Elijah or whom you will; honor followed honor as harvest the seed. The man of God set his heart to exalt God above all; God accepted his intention as fact and acted accordingly. Not perfection, but holy intention made the difference.

In our Lord Jesus Christ this law was seen in simple perfection. In His lowly manhood

God expects of us only what He has Himself first supplied. He is quick to mark every simple effort to please Him, and just as quick to overlook imperfections when He knows we meant to do His will. He loves us for ourselves and values our love more than galaxies of new created worlds.

—AWT in The Root of the Righteous

He humbled Himself and gladly gave all glory to His Father in heaven. He sought not His own honor, but the honor of God who sent Him. "If I honour myself," He said on one occasion, "my honour is nothing: it is my Father that honoureth me" (John 8:54). So far had the Pharisees departed from this law that they could not understand one who honored God at his own expense. "I honour my Father," said Jesus to them, "and ye do dishonour me" (8:49).

It's ludicrous for any Christian to believe that he or she is the worthy object of public worship; it would be like the donkey carrying Jesus into Jerusalem believing the crowds were cheering and laying down their garments for him.
—Charles Colson

Another saying of Jesus, and a most disturbing one, was put in the form of a question. "How can ye believe, which receive honour one of another, and seek not the honour that cometh from God only?" (5:44). If I understand this correctly, Christ taught here the alarming doctrine that the desire for honor among men made belief impossible. Is this sin at the root of religious unbelief? Could it be that those "intellectual difficulties" which men blame for their inability to believe are but smoke screens to conceal the real cause that lies behind them? Was it this greedy desire for honor from man that made men into Pharisees and Pharisees into deicides? Is this the secret back of religious self-righteousness and empty worship? I believe it may be. The whole course of the life is upset by failure to put God where He belongs. We exalt ourselves instead of God and the curse follows.

In our desire after God let us keep always in mind that God also has desire, and His desire is toward the sons of men, and more particularly toward those sons of men who will make the once-for-all decision to exalt Him over all. Such as these are precious to God above all treasures of earth or sea. In them God finds a theater where He can display His exceeding kindness toward us in Christ Jesus. With them God can walk unhindered; toward them He can act like the God He is.

In speaking thus I have one fear: that I may convince the mind before God can win the heart. For this God-above-all position is one not easy to take. The mind may approve it while not having the consent of the will to put it into effect. While the imagination races ahead to honor God, the will may lag behind and the man must make the decision before the heart can know any real satisfaction. God wants the whole person, and He will not rest till He gets us in entirety. No part of the man will do.

Let us pray over this in detail, throwing ourselves at God's feet and meaning everything we say. No one who prays thus in sincerity need wait long for tokens of divine acceptance. God will unveil His glory before His servant's eyes, and He will place all His treasures at the disposal of such a one, for He knows that His honor is safe in such consecrated hands.

> *Rise, O Lord, into Thy proper place of honor, above my ambitions, above my likes and dislikes, above my family, my health and even my life itself. Let me sink that Thou mayest rise above. Ride forth upon me as Thou didst ride into Jerusalem mounted upon the humble little beast, a colt, the foal of an ass, and let me hear the children cry to Thee, "Hosanna in the highest."*

Day 27

Release from Inner Burdens

But the meek shall inherit the earth; and shall delight themselves in the abundance of peace.
Psalm 37:11

For the LORD taketh pleasure in his people: he will beautify the meek with salvation.
Psalm 149:4

The meek will he guide in judgment: and the meek will he teach his way.
Psalm 25:9

A fairly accurate description of the human race might be furnished to one unacquainted with it by taking the Beatitudes, turning them wrong side out and saying, "Here is your human race." For the exact opposite of the virtues in the Beatitudes are the very qualities which distinguish human life and conduct.

In the world of men we find nothing approaching the virtues of which Jesus spoke in the opening words of the famous Sermon on the Mount. Instead of poverty of spirit we find the rankest kind of pride; instead of mourners we find pleasure seekers; instead of meekness, arrogance; instead of hunger after righteousness we hear men saying, "I am rich and increased with goods and have need of nothing"; instead of mercy we find cruelty; instead of purity of heart, corrupt imaginings; instead of peacemakers we find men quarrelsome and resentful; instead of rejoicing in mistreatment we find them fighting back with every weapon at their command.

Of this kind of moral stuff civilized society is composed. The atmosphere is charged with it; we breathe it with every breath and drink it with our mother's milk. Culture and education refine these things slightly but leave them basically untouched. A whole world of literature has been created to justify this kind of life as the only normal one. And this is the more to be wondered at seeing that these are the evils which make life the bitter struggle it is for all of us. All our heartaches and a great many of our physical ills spring directly out of our sins. Pride, arrogance, resentfulness, evil imaginings, malice, greed are the sources of more human pain then all the diseases that ever afflicted mortal flesh.

Into a world like this the sound of Jesus' words comes wonderful and strange, a visitation from above. It is well that He spoke, for no one else could have done it as well; and it is good that we listen. His words are the essence of truth. He is not offering an opinion; Jesus never uttered opinions. He never guessed; He knew, and He knows.

His words are not as Solomon's were, the sum of sound wisdom or the results of keen observation. He spoke out of the fullness of His Godhead, and His words are very Truth itself. He is the only one who could say "blessed" with complete authority, for He is the Blessed One come from the world above to confer blessedness upon mankind. And His words were supported by deeds mightier than any performed on this earth by any other man. It is wisdom for us to listen.

> *The Sermon on the Mount cuts across differences of temperament and variations in capacity. It outlines the kind of character which is possible for any man, gifted or relatively ungifted, strong or weak, clever or slow. Once more we find Christ placing His finger, not upon the externals, but upon the vital internal attitude.*
>
> *—J.B. Phillips*

As was often so with Jesus, He used this word *meek* in a brief crisp sentence, and not till sometime later did He go on to explain it. In the same book of Matthew He tells us more about it and applies it to our lives. "Come unto me, all ye that labour and are heavy laden, and I will give you rest. Take my yoke upon you, and learn of me; for I am meek and lowly in heart: and ye shall find rest unto your souls. For my yoke is easy, and my burden is light" (11:28–30). Here we have two things standing in contrast to each other, a burden and a rest. The burden is not a local one, peculiar to those first hearers, but one which is borne by the whole human race. It consists not of political oppression or poverty or hard work. It is far deeper than that. It is felt by the rich as well as the poor, for it is something from which wealth and idleness can never deliver us.

The burden borne by mankind is a heavy and a crushing thing. The word Jesus used means "a

The People's Beatitudes

Happy are the pushers for they get on in the world.

Happy are the hard-boiled for they never let life hurt them.

Happy are they who complain for they get their own way in the end.

Happy are the blasé for they never worry over their sins.

Happy are the slave drivers for they get results.

Happy are the knowledgeable men of the world for they know their way around.

Happy are the troublemakers for they make people take notice of them.

—J.B. Phillips

load carried or toil borne to the point of exhaustion." Rest is simply release from that burden. It is not something we do; it is what comes to us when we cease to do. His own meekness, that is the rest.

Let us examine our burden. It is altogether an interior one. It attacks the heart and the mind and reaches the body only from within. First, there is the burden of *pride*. The labor of self-love is a heavy one indeed. Think for yourself whether much of your sorrow has not arisen from someone speaking slightingly of you. As long as you set yourself up as a little god to which you must be loyal there will be those who will delight to offer affront to your idol. How then can you hope to have inward peace? The heart's fierce effort to protect itself from every slight, to shield its touchy honor from the bad opinion of friend and enemy, will never let the mind have rest. Continue this fight through the years and the burden will become intolerable. Yet the sons of earth are carrying this burden continually, challenging every word spoken against them, cringing under every criticism, smarting under each fancied slight, tossing sleepless if another is preferred before them.

Such a burden as this is not necessary to bear. Jesus calls us to His rest, and meekness is His method. The meek man cares not at all who is greater than he, for he has long ago decided that the esteem of the world is not worth the effort. He develops toward himself a kindly sense of humor and learns to say, "Oh, so you have been over-looked? They have placed someone else before you? They have whispered that you are pretty small stuff after all? And now you feel hurt because the world is saying about you the very things you have been saying about yourself? Only yesterday you were telling God that you were nothing, a mere worm of the dust. Where is your consistency? Come on, humble yourself and cease to care what men think."

~God's Call to Meekness~

Do all things without murmurings and disputings: That ye may be blameless and harmless, the sons of God, without rebuke, in the midst of a crooked and perverse nation.

Philippians 2:14-15

Bless them which persecute you: bless, and curse not. If it be possible, as much as lieth in you, live peaceably with all men.

Romans 12:14, 18

Put on . . . as the elect of God, holy and beloved, bowels of mercies, kindness, humbleness of mind, meekness, longsuffering; Forbearing one another, and forgiving one another, if any man have a quarrel against any: even as Christ forgave you, so also do ye.

Colossians 3:12-13

Why do ye not rather take wrong? why do ye not rather suffer yourselves to be defrauded?

1 Corinthians 6:7

For ye know the grace of our Lord Jesus Christ, that, though he was rich, yet for your sakes he became poor, that ye through his poverty might be rich.

2 Corinthians 8:9

He was oppressed, and he was afflicted, yet he opened not his mouth: he is brought as a lamb to the slaughter, and as a sheep before her shearers is dumb, so he openeth not his mouth.

Isaiah 53:7

Christ also suffered for us, leaving us an example, that ye should follow his steps: . . . Who, when he was reviled, reviled not again; when he suffered, he threatened not; but committed himself to him that judgeth righteously.

1 Peter 2:21, 23

Not rendering evil for evil, or railing for railing: but contrariwise blessing; knowing that ye are thereunto called, that ye should inherit a blessing.

1 Peter 3:9

Day 28

The Rest of Self-Forgetfulness

Thy home is with the humble, Lord!
The simple are Thy rest;
Thy lodging is in childlike hearts;
Thou makest there Thy rest.
—Frederick W. Faber

The meek man is not a human mouse afflicted with a sense of his own inferiority. Rather, he may be in his moral life as bold as a lion and as strong as Samson; but he has stopped being fooled about himself. He has accepted God's estimate of his own life. He knows he is as weak and helpless as God has declared him to be, but paradoxically, he knows at the same time that he is, in the sight of God, more important than angels. In himself, nothing; in God, everything. That is his motto. He knows well that the world will never see him as God sees him and he has stopped caring. He rests perfectly content to allow God to place His own values. He will be patient to wait for the day when everything will get its own price

179

tag and real worth will come into its own. Then the righteous shall shine forth in the kingdom of their Father. He is willing to wait for that day.

In the meantime, he will have attained a place of soul rest. As he walks on in meekness he will be happy to let God defend him. The old struggle to defend himself is over. He has found the peace which meekness brings.

The humble person has changed humiliation into humility.

—Bernard of Clairvaux

◇ ◇ ◇

*Dear Christ, make one that which we are
and that which we appear to be.
Be Lord of naked faces.
— Calvin Miller*

◇ ◇ ◇

Then also he will get deliverance from the burden of *pretense*. By this I mean not hypocrisy, but the common human desire to put the best foot forward and hide from the world our real inward poverty. For sin has played many evil tricks upon us, and one has been the infusing into us of a false sense of shame. There is hardly a man or woman who dares to be just what he or she is without doctoring up the impression. The fear of being found out gnaws like rodents within their hearts.

The man of culture is haunted by the fear that he will someday come upon a man more cultured than himself. The learned man fears to meet a man more learned than he. The rich man sweats under the fear that his clothes or his car or his house will sometime be made to look cheap by comparison with those of another rich man. So-called "society" runs by a motivation not higher than this, and the poorer classes on their level are little better.

Let no one smile this off. These burdens are real, and little by little they kill the victims of this evil and unnatural way of life. And the psychology created by years of this kind of thing makes true meekness seem as unreal as a dream, as aloof as a star. To all the victims of the gnawing disease Jesus says, "Ye . . . [must] become as little children" (Matthew 18:3). For little children do not compare; they receive direct enjoyment from what they have without relating it to something else or someone else. Only as they get older and sin begins to stir within their hearts do jealousy and envy appear. Then they are unable to enjoy what they have if someone else has something larger or better. At that early age does the galling burden come down upon their tender souls, and it never leaves them till Jesus sets them free.

Another source of burden is *artificiality*. I am sure that most people live in secret fear that some day they will be careless and by chance an enemy or friend will be allowed to peep into their poor, empty souls. So they are never relaxed. Bright people are tense and alert in fear that they may be trapped into saying something common or stupid. Traveled people are afraid that they may meet some Marco Polo who is able to describe some remote place where they have never been.

This unnatural condition is part of our sad heritage of sin, but in our day it is aggravated by our whole way of life. Advertising is largely based upon this habit of pretense. "Courses" are offered in this or that field of human learning frankly appealing to the victim's desire to shine at a party. Books are sold, clothes and cosmetics are peddled by playing continually upon this desire to appear what we are not. Artificiality is one curse that will drop away the moment we kneel at Jesus' feet and surrender ourselves to His meekness. Then we will not care what people think of us so long as God is pleased. Then *what we are* will be everything; what we appear will take its place far down the scale of interest for us. Apart from sin we have nothing of

> *The most fatiguing activity in the world is the drive to seem other than you are; it is less exhausting to become what you want to be than to maintain a facade.*
>
> *—Sydney J. Harris*

which to be ashamed. Only an evil desire to shine makes us want to appear other than we are.

◇ ◇ ◇

I used to think that God's gifts were on shelves one above the other and that the taller we grew in Christian character the more easily we could reach them. I now find that God's gifts are on shelves one beneath the other and that it is not a question of growing taller but of stooping lower.
—F.B. Meyer

◇ ◇ ◇

The heart of the world is breaking under this load of pride and pretense. There is no release from our burden apart from the meekness of Christ. Good, keen reasoning may help slightly, but so strong is the vice that if we push it down one place, it will come up somewhere else. To men and women everywhere Jesus says, "Come unto me, and I will give you rest." The rest He offers is the rest of meekness, the blessed relief which comes when we accept ourselves for what we are

What you possess in the world will be found at the day of your death to belong to someone else, but what you are will be yours forever.

—Henry Van Dyke

and cease to pretend. It will take some courage at first, but the needed grace will come as we learn that we are sharing this new and easy yoke with the strong Son of God Himself. He calls it "my yoke," and He walks at one end while we walk at the other.

Lord, make me childlike. Deliver me from the urge to compete with another for place or prestige or position. I would be simple and artless as a little child. Deliver me from pose and pretense. Forgive me for thinking of myself. Help me to forget myself and find my true peace in beholding Thee. That Thou may answer this prayer I humble myself before Thee. Lay upon me Thy easy yoke of self-forgetfulness that through it I may find rest. Amen.

Unifying the Sacred
and the Secular

Teach me, my God and King,
In all things Thee to see;
And what I do in anything,
To do it as for Thee!

—George Herbert

*O*ne of the greatest hindrances to internal peace which the Christian encounters is the common habit of dividing our lives into two areas—the sacred and the secular. As these areas are conceived to exist apart from each other and to be morally and spiritually incompatible, and as we are compelled by the necessities of living to be always crossing back and forth from the one to the other, our inner lives tend to break up so that we live a divided instead of a unified life.

Our trouble springs from the fact that we who follow Christ inhabit at once two worlds—the spiritual and the natural. As children of Adam we live our lives on earth subject to the limitations of the flesh and the weaknesses and ills to which human nature is heir. Merely to live among men requires of us years of hard toil and much care and attention to the things of this world. In sharp contrast to this is our life in the Spirit. There we enjoy another and higher kind of life—we are children of God; we possess heavenly status and enjoy intimate fellowship with Christ.

This tends to divide our total life into two departments. We come unconsciously to recognize two sets of actions. The first are performed with a feeling of satisfaction and a firm assurance that they are pleasing to God. These are the sacred acts and they are usually thought to be prayer, Bible reading, hymn singing, church attendance and such other acts as spring directly from faith. They may be known by the fact that they have no direct relation to this world, and would have no meaning whatever except as faith shows us another world, "an house not made with hands, eternal in the heavens" (2 Corinthians 5:1).

Over against these sacred acts are the secular ones. They include all of the ordinary activities of life which we share with the sons and daughters of Adam: eating, sleeping, working, looking after the needs of the body and performing our dull and prosaic duties here on earth. These we often do reluctantly and with many misgivings, often apologizing to God for what we consider a waste of time and strength. The upshot of this is that we are uneasy most of the time. We go about our common tasks with a feeling of deep frustration, telling ourselves pensively that there's a better day coming when we shall slough off this earthly shell and be bothered no more with the affairs of this world.

> Monday-through-Friday employment is pure, it's sacred—just as sacred as your Sunday activities.
>
> —Charles R. Swindoll

This is the old sacred-secular antithesis. Most Christians are caught in its trap. They cannot get a satisfactory adjustment between the claims of the two worlds. They try to walk the tightrope between two kingdoms and they find no peace in either. Their strength is reduced, their outlook confused and their joy taken from them.

I believe this state of affairs to be wholly unnecessary. We have gotten ourselves on the horns of a dilemma, true enough, but the dilemma is not real. It is a creature of misunderstanding. The sacred-secular antithesis has no foundation in the New Testament. Without doubt, a more perfect understanding of Christian truth will deliver us from it.

◊   ◊   ◊

Do little things as if they were great because
of the majesty of the Lord Jesus Christ

*who dwells in you; and do
great things
as if they were little and
easy
because of His omnipotence.*
—Blaise Pascal

◇   ◇   ◇

The Lord Jesus Christ Himself is our perfect example, and He knew no divided life. In the presence of His Father He lived on earth without strain from babyhood to His death on the cross. God accepted the offering of His total life and made no distinction between act and act. "I do always those things that please him," was His brief summary of His own life as it related to the Father (John 8:29). As He moved among men He was poised and restful. What pressure and suffering He endured grew out of His position as the world's sin bearer; they were never the result of moral uncertainty or spiritual maladjustment.

Who is the greatest saint in the world? It is not he who prays most or fasts most; it is not he who gives most alms, or is most eminent for temperance, chastity, or justice; but it is he who is always thankful to God, who wills everything that God wills, who receives everything as an instance of God's goodness, and has a heart always ready to praise God for it.

—William Law

◊   ◊   ◊

Drop Thy still dews of
quietness,
Till all our strivings cease;
Take from our souls the strain and stress,
And let our ordered lives confess
The beauty of Thy peace.

Breathe thro' the heats of our desire
Thy coolness and Thy balm;
Let sense be dumb, let flesh retire;
Speak thro' the earthquake, wind and fire,
O still small voice of calm.
—John G. Whittier

◊   ◊   ◊

Day 30

The Sacredness
of the Human Body

*Present your bodies a living sacrifice, holy,
acceptable unto God, which is your reason-
able service.*

Romans 12:1

*Know ye not that your body is the temple of the
Holy Ghost which is in you, which ye have of
God, and ye are not your own? For ye are
bought with a price: therefore glorify God in
your body, and in your spirit, which are God's.*

1 Corinthians 6:19-20

*Whether therefore ye eat, or drink, or what-
soever ye do, do all to the glory of God.*

1 Corinthians 10:31

*P*aul's exhortation to "do all to the glory of God" is more than pious idealism. It is an integral part of the sacred revelation and is to be accepted as the very Word of Truth. It opens before us the possibility of making every act of our lives contribute to the glory of God. Lest we should be too timid to include everything, Paul mentions specifically eating and drinking. This humble privilege we share with the beasts that perish. If these lowly animal acts can be so performed as to honor God, then it becomes difficult to conceive of one that cannot.

> *For every creature of God is good, and nothing to be refused, if it be received with thanksgiving: For it is sanctified by the word of God and prayer.*
>
> 1 Timothy 4:4-5

Our body is the most gracious gift God has given us, and if we hand over the mainspring of our life to God we can work out in our bodily life all that He works in. It is through our bodily lives that Satan works, and, thank God, it is through our bodily lives that God's Spirit works. God gives us His grace and His Spirit; He puts right all that was wrong, He does not suppress it nor counteract it, but readjusts the whole thing; then begins our work.
— Oswald Chambers

That monkish hatred of the body which figures so prominently in the works of certain early devotional writers is wholly without support in the Word of God. Common modesty is found in the sacred Scriptures, it is true, but never prudery or a false sense of shame. The New Testament accepts as a matter of course that in His incarnation our Lord took upon Him a real human body, and no effort is made to steer around the downright implications of such a fact. He lived in that body here among men and never once performed a non-sacred act. His presence in human flesh sweeps away forever the evil notion that there is about the human body something innately offensive to the Deity. God created our bodies, and we do not offend Him by placing the responsibility where it belongs. He is not ashamed of the work of His own hands.

> *Christianity is almost the only one of the great religions which thoroughly approves of the body— which believes that matter is good, that God Himself once took on a human body, that some kind of body is going to be given to us even in heaven and is going to be an essential part of our happiness, our beauty, and our energy.*
>
> *— C.S. Lewis*

Perversion, misuse and abuse of our human powers should give us cause enough to be ashamed. Bodily acts done in sin and contrary to nature can never honor God. Wherever the human will introduces moral evil we have no longer our innocent and harmless powers as God made them; we have instead an abused and twisted thing which can never bring glory to its Creator.

Let us, however, assume that perversion and abuse are not present. Let us think of a Christian believer in whose life the twin wonders of repentance and the new birth have been wrought. He is now living according to the will of God as he understands it from the written Word. Of such a one it may be said that every act of his life is or can be as truly sacred as prayer or baptism or the Lord's Supper. To say this is not to bring all acts down to one dead level; it

It is not only prayer that gives God glory but work. Smiting on an anvil, sawing a beam, whitewashing a wall, driving horses, sweeping, scouring, everything gives God glory if believing in His grace you do it as your duty. To go to Communion worthily gives God great glory, but to take food in thankfulness and temperance gives Him glory too. To lift up the hands in prayer gives God glory, but a man with a dungfork in his hand, a woman with a slop pail, gives Him glory too. He is so great that all things give Him glory if you mean they should.

— Gerard Manley Hopkins

is rather to lift every act up into a living kingdom and turn the whole life into a sacrament.

If a sacrament is an external expression of an inward grace, then we need not hesitate to accept the above thesis. By one act of consecration of our total selves to God we can make every subsequent act express that consecration. We need no more be ashamed of our body—the fleshly servant that carries us through life—than Jesus was of the humble beast upon which He rode into Jerusalem. "The Lord hath need of [him]" (Matthew 21:3) may well apply to our mortal bodies. If Christ dwells in us, we may bear about the Lord of glory as the little beast did of old and give occasion to the multitudes to cry, "Hosanna in the highest."

That we *see* this truth is not enough. If we would escape from the toils of the sacred-secular dilemma, the truth must "run in our blood" and condition the complex of our thoughts. We must practice living to the glory of God, actually and determinedly. By meditation upon this truth, by talking it over with God often in our prayers, by recalling it to our minds frequently as we move about among men, a sense of its wondrous meaning will take hold of us. The old painful duality will go down before a restful unity of life. The knowledge that we are all God's, that He has received all and rejected nothing, will unify our inner lives and make everything sacred to us.

All to Jesus I surrender;
Humbly at His feet I bow,
Worldly pleasures all forsaken.
Take me, Jesus, take me now.

All to Jesus I surrender;
Make me, Saviour, wholly Thine;
Let me feel the Holy Spirit,
Truly know that Thou art mine.
—*Judson W. Van De Venter*

Day 31

The Sacredness of Everyday Living

There is no work better than another to please God; to pour water, to wash dishes, to be a cobbler, or an apostle, all is one; to wash dishes and to preach is all one to please God.

—William Tyndale

*L*ong-held habits do not die easily. It will take intelligent thought and a great deal of reverent prayer to escape completely from the sacred-secular psychology. For instance, it may be difficult for the average Christian to get hold of the idea that his daily labors can be performed as acts of worship acceptable to God by Jesus Christ. The old antithesis will crop up in the back of his head sometimes to disturb his peace of mind. Nor will that old serpent, the devil, take all this lying down. He will be there in the cab or at the desk or in the field to remind the Christian that he is giving the better part of his day to the things of this world and allotting to his religious duties only a trifling portion of his time. And unless great care is taken, this will create confusion and bring discouragement and heaviness of heart.

We can meet this successfully only by the exercise of an aggressive faith. We must offer all our acts to God and believe that He accepts them. Then hold firmly to that position and keep insisting that every act of every hour of the day and night be included in the transaction. Keep reminding God in our times of private prayer that we mean every act for His glory; then supplement those times by a thousand thought-prayers as we go about the job of living. Let us practice the fine art of making every work a priestly ministration. Let us believe that God is in all our simple deeds and learn to find Him there.

> Lord, turn the routines of work into celebrations of love.
>
> —Unknown

A concomitant of the error which we have been discussing is the sacred-secular antithesis as applied to places. It is little short of astonishing that we can read the New Testament and still believe in the inherent sacredness of some places. This error is so widespread that one feels all alone when he tries to combat it. It has acted as a kind of dye to color the thinking of religious persons and has colored the eyes as well so that it is all but impossible to detect its fallacy. In the face of every New

Testament teaching to the contrary, it has been said and sung throughout the centuries and accepted as a part of the Christian message, the which it most surely is not. Only the Quakers, so far as my knowledge goes, have had the perception to see the error and the courage to expose it.

Here are the facts as I see them. For 400 years Israel had dwelt in Egypt, surrounded by the crassest idolatry. By the hand of Moses they were brought out at last and started toward the land of promise. The very idea of holiness had been lost to them. To correct this, God began at the bottom. He localized Himself in the cloud and fire, and later when the tabernacle had been built He dwelt in fiery manifestation in the Holy of Holies. By innumerable distinctions God taught Israel the difference between holy and unholy. There were holy days, holy vessels, holy garments. There were washings, sacrifices, offerings of many kinds. By these means, Israel learned that *God is holy*. It was this that He was teaching them, not the holiness of things or

> We can do little things for God: I turn the cake that is frying on the pan, for love of Him; and that done, if there is nothing else to call me, I prostrate myself in worship before Him who has given me grace to work; afterward I rise happier than a king.
>
> —Brother Lawrence

places. The holiness of Jehovah was the lesson they must learn.

Then came the great day when Christ appeared. Immediately He began to say, "Ye have heard that it was said by them of old time . . . but *I* say unto you" (Matthew 5:21–22). The Old Testament schooling was over. When Christ died on the cross, the veil of the temple was rent from top to bottom. The Holy of Holies was opened to everyone who would enter in faith. Christ's words were remembered, "The hour cometh, when ye shall neither in this mountain, nor yet at Jerusalem, worship the Father. . . . But the hour cometh, and now is, when the true worshippers shall worship the Father in spirit and in truth: for the Father seeketh such to worship him. God is a Spirit: and they that worship him must worship him in spirit and in truth" (John 4:21, 23–24).

Shortly after, Paul took up the cry of liberty and declared all meats clean, every day holy, all places sacred and every act acceptable to God. The sacredness of times and places, a half-light necessary to the education of the race, passed away before the full sun of spiritual worship.

The essential spirituality of worship remained the possession of the Church until it was slowly lost with the passing of the years. Then the natural *legality* of the fallen hearts of men began to introduce the old distinctions. The Church came to observe again days and seasons and times. Certain places were chosen and marked out as holy in a special sense. Differences were observed between one and another day or place or person. "The sacraments" were first two, then three, then four, until with the triumph of Romanism they were fixed at seven.

In all charity, and with no desire to reflect unkindly upon any Christian, however misled, I would point out that the Roman Catholic Church represents today the sacred-secular heresy carried to its logical conclusion. Its deadliest effect is the complete cleavage it introduces between religion and life. Its teachers attempt to avoid this snare by many footnotes and multitudinous explanations, but the mind's instinct for logic is too strong. In practical living the cleavage is a fact.

From this bondage reformers and puritans and mystics have labored to free us. Today, the trend in conservative circles is back toward that bondage again. It is said that a horse, after it has been led out of a burning building, will sometimes, by a strange obstinacy, break loose from its rescuer and dash back into the building again to perish in the flame. By some such stubborn tendency toward error, fundamentalism in our day is moving back toward spiritual slavery. The observation of days and times is becoming more and more prominent among us. "Lent" and "holy week" and "good" Friday are words heard more and more frequently upon the lips of gospel Christians. We do not know when we are well off.

Christianity is neither contemplation nor action. It is participation. Contemplation is looking at God as if He were an object. But if you participate in God in the sense that you let yourself be penetrated by Him, you will go to the cross like Him, you will go to work like Him, you will clean shoes, do the washing up and the cooking, all like Him.
You cannot do otherwise because you will have become part of Him. You will do what He loves to do.
—Louis Evely

In order that I may be understood and not be misunderstood, I would throw into relief the practical implications of the teaching for which I have been arguing, i.e., the sacramental quality of everyday living. Over against its positive meanings, I should like to point out a few things it does not mean.

It does not mean, for instance, that everything we do is of equal importance with everything else we do or may do. One act of a good man's life may differ widely from another in importance. Paul's sewing of tents was not equal to his writing of an

Epistle to the Romans, but both were accepted of God and both were true acts of worship. Certainly it is more important to lead a soul to Christ than to plant a garden, but the planting of the garden *can* be as holy an act as the winning of a soul.

Again, it does not mean that every man is as useful as every other man. Gifts differ in the body of Christ. A Billy Bray is not to be compared with a Luther or a Wesley for sheer usefulness to the church and to the world; but the service of the less gifted brother is as pure as that of the more gifted, and God accepts both with equal pleasure.

The "layman" need never think of his humbler task as being inferior to that of his minister. Let every man abide in the calling wherein he is called and his work will be as sacred as the work of

Where is the church at 11:25 on Monday morning? The church then is in the dentist's office, in the automobile sales room and repair shop, and out in the truck. It is in the hospital, in the classroom, and in the home. It is in the offices, insurance, law, real estate, whatever it is. That is where the church is, wherever God's people are. They are doing what they ought to be doing. They are honoring God, not just while they worship in a building but out there.

—Arthur H. DeKruyter

the ministry. It is not what a man does that determines whether his work is sacred or secular, it is *why* he does it. The motive is everything. Let a man sanctify the Lord God in his heart and he can thereafter do no common act. All he does is good and acceptable to God through Jesus Christ. For such a man, living itself will be a priestly ministration. As he performs his never-so-simple task, he will hear the voice of the seraphim saying, "Holy, holy, holy, is the LORD of hosts: the whole earth is full of his glory" (Isaiah 6:3).

Lord, I would trust Thee completely; I would be altogether Thine; I would exalt Thee above all. I desire that I may feel no sense of possessing anything outside of Thee. I want constantly to be aware of Thy overshadowing presence and to hear Thy speaking voice. I long to live in restful sincerity of heart. I want to live so fully in the Spirit that all my thoughts may be as sweet incense ascending to Thee and every act of my life may be an act of worship. Therefore I pray in the words of Thy great servant of old, "I beseech Thee so for to cleanse the intent of mine heart with the unspeakable gift of Thy grace, that I may perfectly love Thee and worthily praise Thee." And all this I confidently believe Thou wilt grant me through the merits of Jesus Christ Thy Son. Amen.

Sources Cited

Most of the quotations in this book are from *Draper's Book of Quotations for the Christian World* by Edythe Draper and are quoted with permission from Tyndale House Publishers (Wheaton, IL: 1992).

All quotations from A.W. Tozer are from Christian Publications:

Born After Midnight, © 1989.
The Divine Conquest, © 1978.
God Tells the Man Who Cares, © 1992.
I Call It Heresy!, © 1991.
I Talk Back to the Devil, © 1990.
Man: The Dwelling Place of God, © 1966.
The Next Chapter After the Last, © 1987.
Of God and Men, © 1995.
That Incredible Christian, © 1964.
The Root of the Righteous, © 1986.
Who Put Jesus on the Cross?, © 1975.

Additional sources cited:

Bathurst, William. (p. 78) from *Hymns of the Christian Life* (Camp Hill, PA: Christian Publications, 1978), #151.

Bonar, Horatius. (p. 50) from *Hymns of the Christian Life*, #429.

Brent, Charles H. (p. 107) from *Joy and Strength* (Minneapolis, MN: World Wide Publications, 1986), January 14 reading.

Brook, F. (p. 141) from *Hymns of the Christian Life*, #264.
    (p. 146) from *Hymns of the Christian Life*, #264.

Cowper, William. (p. 72) from *Worship and Service Hymnal* (Carol Stream, IL: Hope Publishing Co., 1957), #353.
    (p. 123) from *Hymns of the Christian Life*, #409.

Croly, George. (pp. 100-101) from *Hyms of the Christian Life*, #137.

Faber, Frederick. (pp. 4-5) from *The Christian Book of Mystical Verse* (Camp Hill, PA: Christian Publications, 1991), pp. 51-52.
    (p. 59) from *Joy and Strength*, August 31 reading.

Grimes, E. May. (p. 121) from *Hyms of the Christian Life*, #205.

Guyon, Jeanne. (p. 16) from *Final Steps in Christian Maturity* (Auburn, ME: Christian Books

Publishing House, 1985. Taken from excerpts of a larger, three-volume work entitled *Justifications*. These excerpts were first published in English privately by George W. McCall in 1915), p. 102.

Hamilton, Anna E. (p. 133) from *Joy and Strength*, October 1 reading.

Hatch, Edwin. (p. 57) from *Hymns of the Christian Life*, #139.

Lambert, D.W. (p. 62) from *Topical Encyclopedia of Living Quotations* (Minneapolis, MN: Bethany House, 1982), p. 110.

Lawrence, Brother. (p. 90) from *The Practice of the Presence of God* (Springdale, PA: Whittaker House, 1982), p. 59-60.
          (p. 136) from *The Practice of the Presence of God*, p. 64.

Liddon, Henry Parry. (p. 60) from *Joy and Strength*, November 19 reading.

Morris, Lelia N. (p. 96) from *Hymns of the Christian Life*, #295.

Murray, Andrew. (p. 47) from *Joy and Strength*, February 10 reading.

Runyan, William M. (pp. 113-114) from *Hymns of the Christian Life*, #208.

Snead, A.C. (pp. 31-32) from *Hymns of the Christian Life*, #218.

Swain, Joseph. (p. 41) from *Worship and Service Hymnal*, #370.

Tersteegen, Gerhard. (p. 14) from *The Christian Book of Mystical Verse*, pp. 72-73.

Van De Venter, Judson W. (p. 196) from *Hymns of the Christian Life*, #216.

Whittier, John G. (p. 189) from *Hymns of the Christian Life*, #154.